ANCHOR HOCKING'S

Fire-King & MORE

SECOND EDITION

IDENTIFICATION & VALUE GUIDE

Including Early American Prescut and Wexford

COLLECTOR BOOKS

A Division of Schroeder Publishing Co., Inc.

GENE FLORENCE

ABOUT THE AUTHOR

Gene Florence, Jr., born in Lexington in 1944, graduated from the University of Kentucky where he held a double major in mathematics and English. He taught for nine years in Kentucky at the junior high and high school levels before his glass collecting "hobby" became his full-time job.

Mr. Florence has been interested in collecting since childhood, beginning with baseball cards and progressing through comic books, coins, bottles and finally, glassware. He first became interested in Depression glassware after purchasing an entire set of Sharon dinnerware for $5.00 at a garage sale.

He has written several books on glassware: *The Collector's Encyclopedia of Depression Glass*, in its fourteenth edition; *Florence's Glassware Pattern Identification Guide*, Volumes I and II; *Kitchen Glassware of the Depression Years*, in its fifth edition with updated values; *Elegant Glassware of the Depression Era*, in its ninth edition; *The Collector's Encyclopedia of Akro Agate*, now out of print; *The Collector's Encyclopedia of Occupied Japan*, Volumes I, II, III, IV, V, and Price Guide Update Series 1–5; *Very Rare Glassware of the Depression Years*, Volumes I, II, III, IV, V, and VI; the *Pocket Guide to Depression Glass*, now in its twelfth edition; and *Collectible Glassware from the 40s, 50s, 60s....* He also authored six editions of a baseball book that is now out of print as well as a book on Degenhart for that museum.

His Grannie Bear Antique Shop in Lexington, Kentucky, closed in 1993, due to the death of his beloved mother, "Grannie Bear," who managed that store. However, Mr. Florence continues to sell glassware at Depression glass shows throughout the country as well as via mail order or his web page (www.geneflorence.com). Currently, considerable time is spent in Florida where writing is easier without the phone ringing every five minutes — and fishing is just out the office door!

If you know of unlisted or unusual pieces of glassware in the patterns shown in this book, you may write him at Box 22186, Lexington, KY 40522, or at Box 64, Astatula, FL 34705. If you expect a reply, please enclose a SASE (self-addressed, stamped envelope) — and be patient. Very little mail is answered between Christmas and the middle of May due to his writing, research, and travel schedule. This often causes a backlog of the hundreds of letters he receives weekly. He appreciates your interest and input and spends many hours answering letters when time and circumstances permit which is often on plane trips or in motel rooms across the country. Remember that SASE! He does not open mail. Most letters without a SASE are never seen by him!

From the Front Cover: Christmas mug, $20.00 – 25.00; Colonial Kitchen Jade-ite bowls, 6", $70.00 – 75.00, 7³⁄₁₆", $90.00 – 100.00, 8¾", $90.00 – 100.00; Forest Green Ashtray, NPA; Early American goblet, "Neptune's Table," $25.00; Lace Edge "Distlefink" salad plate, $35.00.

From the Back Cover: Tulip mixing bowls on Ivory, 3 qt., $25.00 – 27.50, 2qt., $20.00 – 22.50, 1qt., $20.00 – 22.50; box, $45.00, 4 qt., $27.50 – 30.00.

From Page 1: Tulip mixing bowl on Ivory, 4 qt., $27.50 – 30.00; "Rainbow" primary colors, assorted pieces (see pgs. 68 – 72).

Cover Design: Beth Summers   Book Design: Terri Hunter and Beth Ray

COLLECTOR BOOKS
P.O. Box 3009
Paducah, Kentucky 42002-3009
www.collectorbooks.com

or

GENE FLORENCE
P.O. Box 22186   P.O. Box 64
Lexington, KY 40522   Astatula, FL 34705

Copyright © 2000 by Gene Florence

Contents

Acknowledgments

Writing a second book is supposed to be easier than the first or so my publisher has jokingly informed me. Without hesitation, I can tell you, it is not so. Rounding up newly discovered Fire-King pieces and adding new patterns became my sole responsibility since the first book's coordinator moved from sunny Florida to the Northeast. I made quite a few trips to Ohio and beyond to obtain additional pieces to photograph. I am grateful to Marianne Jackson and Barbara Wolf of Anchor Hocking who helped me with glassware from the morgue, enabling you to see some very unusual items.

Praises go to Shirley Moore and Beckye Richardson who volunteered to come back to the photography session for the second book after being at the first one! They borrowed boxes of Fire-King from their numerous collector friends and brought a carload full to Paducah. Jeffrey Snyder, an enthusiastic Fire-King collector, who had offered to help me with my next book, really overwhelmed me with the scope of his assistance. He brought a Jeep load of Fire-King, removing the seats and stacking wrapped pieces all around him! It was a sight to behold! I have been loading cars and vans for years and I was impressed! Initially, I had thought we could work out all the new photographs in a couple of days. After Jeff's arrival, it took four long days; but the book is ever so much better for it! We all owe these dedicated collectors much for their efforts to teach us about Fire-King.

A special thanks goes to all the people who contributed both to the first and second book. Valuable Fire-King and information were obtained from Philip Bee, Russ and Susan Allen, Dick and Verylene Summers, Angela Masloff, Mike Kury, Dale Kilgo, Gail Wilkins, Art Moore, Charlie and Peggy McIntosh, Kellie Davison, Marla Vander Werff, Bonnie Koeninger, Jean Spaulding, Dolores Grantham, Geri Jackson, Dan Tucker, Jo Humppi, Carl Streight, LaVella Johnson, Eric and Jaye Fralick, Darrell and Ellie Weikle, Kathy Lynch, Kelvin Kamm, Bill Donofrio, Calvin and Gwen Key, David and Sarah Vandalsem, Randy and Dixie Hardesty, and Mike and Carol LeMay. Ron Marks, a friend from northern Kentucky, went beyond the call of duty to help me find additional Fire-King. These dealers and collectors have willingly shared their expertise and collections with me in order to add to the body of knowledge for everyone. If I have omitted anyone, please forgive me as I have tried to acknowledge each person who had a part in this production.

Cathy, my wife, always encourages the addition of new patterns to my books; so, we have added as many new patterns as we could possibly fit. She has toiled long hours in her capacity of helpmate, proofreader, and "general flunky" as she terms it.

Photographs for this book were realized by Richard Walker of New York and Charles R. Lynch of Collector Books. They provided hundreds of photographs during a seven-day session of which four days involved Fire-King alone. Glass arranging, unpacking, sorting, carting, and repacking was accomplished by Jane White, Zibby Walker, and, as previously mentioned, Cathy, Shirley, Beckye, and Jeff. Van and glass unloading were aided by Billy Schroeder and a couple of Collector Books' shipping crew. We all owe much to this cheerful, competent, and very proficient group of wonderful people.

Thanks, too, to Cathy's parents, Charles and Sibyl, who helped shelve, sort, list, and pack glass for photography and shows. Chad, my eldest son, took time from lateral drilling to help Cathy move, load, and unload boxes of glass; Marc, my youngest son, teaching in the world of computer technology, sees that my web page is available when you look for it at www.geneflorence.com.

Special people to thank in the editorial department at Collector Books include Terri Hunter, Della Maze, Beth Summers, Beth Ray, and Lisa Stroup. Terri translated my e-mail and all those photographs into this book! They have worked diligently to achieve my aspirations of having this book ready for the third Fire-King Expo in Tulsa in May of 2000. Two years ago, we rushed so much, the first book was a month early! Hopefully, this one will not be late!

This is not just *my* book; it is, indeed, a collaborative effort. We hope you enjoy all our endeavors.

Preface

It took only ten months from starting the first Fire-King book until its debut in print. That means starting to buy and borrow glassware as well as accumulate all the information contained therein. It is the shortest time I have ever started from scratch on a new book until it was available for sale. It was quickly adopted by collectors! Two years of buying more Fire-King and meeting new collectors has resulted in this second edition. I am more knowledgeable about the intricacies of Fire-King than I was when the first book was written, but I still do not claim to know as much as collectors who have been buying and collecting it for years. This time I knew the right questions to ask.

Writing this second book required digging deeper and researching more. I have eliminated many of the catalog pages shown in the first book in order to show supplementary patterns and newly found pieces in the patterns in the first book. You will have to find a copy of that first book if you are interested in seeing the way that many of the patterns were advertised and cataloged. Remember, first editions of books become collectible themselves! (My first Depression glass book is now selling for about $200.00 in mint condition!)

Most collectors enjoy sharing their glass and information with others. However, Fire-King collectors seem to share their collections more enthusiastically than any other group that I have worked with in my 29 years of writing! Several wrote to volunteer their "Forget Me Not" sugar bowls to photograph for this book. I had never seen one and neither had anyone I worked with on the first book. Thank you for the letters and confirming pictures. Now, if someone will just find a boxed set so we can discover the real name of the pattern.

The gathering at Collector Books last October was a sight to behold. So many pieces were there that did not make the first book that our allotted photography time doubled. Collectors and dealers brought or shipped glass from Texas, Oklahoma, Florida, Ohio, Kentucky, Minnesota, Illinois, Louisiana, California, New Jersey, Arkansas, and Maryland in addition to all that Cathy and I had been able to locate at various markets throughout the last two years. Those collectors who helped have all said they have a better understanding and appreciation for what I do, but they mostly only saw the fun part! (There were a lot of giggles while cleaning glass with the "rag.") Every one of them is already planning on the next book. Personally, I am just glad to be finishing this one, knowing that there are several more books to get to press before I can think of a third Fire-King.

My eighteen hour days and inevitable aging are beginning to slow me down. So, Cathy and I have decided to limit our show activity and be more active on the Internet (www.geneflorence.com) with mail order than we have been in the past.

I regret this, but another of the things I will be slowing is my answering of letters. In the past, I have asked that questions be limited to patterns in my books. Very few do that, and the Internet and U.S. mail are just overpowering me! I will try to continue answering requests that follow the guidelines, when I get the time. I will no longer even try to identify every picture of glassware sent me. I definitely will *not* go through the stacks of photos sent asking, "What is it; what is it worth; and where can I sell it?" In that regard, I have tried to show and identify much of what I've received letters regarding in two new *Pattern Identification* books I've written. You should look there to find unknown glassware items. These *Pattern Identification* books should save you research time and writing letters. After you find a pattern, and if you want to learn more, you can then look for one of the books in the Bibliography for more information. The likelihood of your having a Depression era pattern that is not in one of these books will be slim. Most of the available "named" patterns are covered there. You are getting years of learning in two books.

Introduction

This book is concerned with Anchor Hocking's Fire-King and their other patterns produced during the same 1940 – 1976 era. Many dealers were slow, at first, to acknowledge the Fire-King collecting phenomenon that had been gaining momentum the past few years; but most are starting to catch up. In 1992, when I added a few Fire-King patterns to my first edition of *Collectible Glassware of the 40s, 50s, 60s...*, I heard some mutterings about waste of space and worthless junk. My objective was to acknowledge that Fire-King was beginning to evoke the same excitement from collectors that Depression glass did in 1972 when I wrote that first book. I try to follow glassware collecting trends to keep books current! Kitchen and Elegant glassware books were born from those observations. I greatly appreciate the reading public who have responded so eagerly to my "lost mind" in the vernacular of some fellow dealers!

Almost every family had some Depression glass around in the early 1970s; and today, pieces of Fire-King are found. Many families are still serving morning coffee and toast from Fire-King. You may have grown up eating with, drinking from, or cooking the meat loaf in Fire-King. My mom's bread pudding was always baked in half a large Sapphire blue roaster. We used other pieces of Fire-King; but seeing that piece out, today, still brings back fond memories. Fifty years of use has generated many followers.

Though you may remember Sapphire blue fondly, it is Jade-ite that has catapulted Fire-King to the collecting forefront. Between the Internet sales and its being seen on television, there has been an awakening of gigantic proportions. To be a "hot" collectible, an item has to be recognizable and plentiful enough for a large quantity of collectors to be able to acquire some pieces. Fire-King Jade-ite fits both of those requirements. Jade-ite was produced around the clock for years. There are millions of pieces out there. The only concern for collectors is condition. This was everyday glassware used in home, restaurants, churches, and military bases. It is very available; but much of it is scratched or worn. Be aware of that when you are buying; someday you may want to sell it.

I have had more letters about Fire-King than anything else in the last two years. Collectors of Early American Prescut in my *Collectible Glassware from the 40s, 50s, 60s...* book have deluged me with letters on that pattern as well as the newer Wexford line. Many collectors assumed these patterns would be collectible and have been quietly hoarding them for years! By the way, if you should have further knowledge regarding any patterns in this book, please write so I may share it with other collectors. The more I learn, the more I realize the magnitude of what still is to be discovered! There are many unofficial names to be found for some of the patterns. Maybe you can be the one to enlighten us as to the real ones.

PRICING

All prices in this book are retail prices for *mint condition* glassware. This book is intended to be only a guide to prices as there are some regional price differences that cannot reasonably be dealt with herein!

You may expect dealers to pay from 40% to 60% less than the prices cited. Glass that is in less than mint condition, i.e., chipped, cracked, scratched, or poorly molded, will bring only a *small* percentage of the price of glass that is in mint condition. This is especially true in the Fire-King collecting field. Some collectors are going to the extreme of buying only labeled items or boxed sets.

Prices are rapidly becoming standardized due to national advertising by dealers, glass shows that are held from coast to coast, and now, the Internet. You can even find me there at www.geneflorence.com. Nationally known dealers and collectors from various regions of the country have assisted in pricing this book. However, there will be some regional price differences on Fire-King due to glass being more readily available in some areas than in others. Anchor Hocking distributed certain pieces in some areas that they did not in others. Generally speaking, price trends are about the same from coast to coast. The Internet makes that an even smaller distance than it once was.

Prices tend to increase faster on rare items; but, in general, they have increased as a whole due to more and more collectors entering the field and people becoming more aware of Fire-King's collectibility. Pricing tends to level off after large increases such as those noted in the last two years; and that is where the market is, today, in early 2000.

One of the more important aspects of this book is the attempt made to illustrate as well as realistically price those items that are in demand. The desire is to give you the most accurate guide to collecting Fire-King available.

MEASUREMENTS

All measurements in this book are exact as to Anchor Hocking's listing or to actual measurement. You may expect variances of up to ½" or 1 – 5 ounces. This may be due to mould variations as moulds wore and were reworked or actual changes by Anchor Hocking. Measurements for catalog listings were often not exact.

"ALICE" 1945 – 1949

Colors: Vitrock, Jade-ite, Vitrock/blue trim, Vitrock/red trim

Every piece available in "Alice" is shown here. The evasive red-trimmed pieces are difficult to find and are missing from most collections. Thanks to a munificent collector of Fire-King, I am able to show them in this edition. (I will not reiterate my diatribe about trying to locate my three pieces that were bought for the first edition of this book.)

Shown are two distinct shades of Vitrock, Hocking's name for their opaque white or beige color. You might find dinner plates to match each of the hues illustrated by the cup and saucers, but many collectors are willing to collect whichever tint they find.

Color variations make it difficult to buy via mail order unless you specifically tell the seller whether you have the light or dark shade of Vitrock. (Your tastes may be different from my Cathy's, who avoids anything beige. That gets really tricky these days, when trying to find a car interior other than beige!

Few sought patterns in the glass collecting field have only three known pieces. "Alice" is an exception. We rarely attend a glass show without someone asking for "Alice" should we not have any visible!

Dinner plates remain difficult pieces to find in "Alice." Evidently, few families bought the plates to go with the free cup and saucers that were packed in oatmeal boxes. Add to that the fact that this was used daily in many households — for years! Many dinner plates found show the wear and tear from all the meals served on them. It seems that this pattern, along with "Jane Ray," was a staple dinnerware in many areas of the country.

	Vitrock	Jade-ite	Vitrock/ blue trim	Vitrock/ red trim
Cup	5.00	7.00	10.00	30.00
Plate, 9½"	20.00	28.00	30.00	60.00
Saucer	2.00	3.00	4.00	15.00

Dinnerware & Patterns

ANNIVERSARY ROSE 1964 – 1965

Colors: White w/decals

Anniversary Rose has attracted many new collectors since its exposure in the first book on Fire-King. Some are finding that an Anniversary Rose collection is nearly as difficult to cultivate in mint condition as real roses. For avid collectors there is a genuine treat on page 10. Take a look at the only known mixing bowl set as well as a separate decaled mixing bowl with vertical decals instead of the traditional horizontal ones. If anyone else should have mixing bowls, let me know. We would like to determine which style is more available. I suspect these were very limited; and since these were found in Lancaster, Ohio, they may even be from an experimental run. I probably saw these in Lancaster when I was first working on the Fire-King book, but did not realize how rare they were at the time. I did not make the same mistake twice.

Anniversary Rose was only pictured in Anchor Hocking's catalogs for two years; so, many pieces are in short supply. I am finding very few pieces that are not worn, faded, and scratched. Gold trims are almost non existent if the dishes were used at all. Automatic dishwashers and strong soaps with lemon additives are a detriment to gold trims and decaled patterns of this era. **Gold has to be mint** for pieces to command the prices listed!

Anniversary mugs seek anonymity from many collectors. Additionally, the platter, chili bowl, and vegetable bowl are not uncovered in any quantity. If you enjoy this attractive, but small set, now is the time to latch on to it before the demise of its short supply.

Collectors of Fire-King prize original boxes! Boxed sets are fetching big prices if the boxes are **colorful and in mint condition**. Box prices alone run from $15.00 for snack sets to $35.00 for dinner sets.

Dinnerware & Patterns

	White w/decals
Bowl, 4⅝", dessert	8.00
Bowl, 5", chili	15.00
Bowl, 6⅝", soup plate	18.00
Bowl, 8¼", vegetable	25.00
Bowl, mixing, 1½ qt.	45.00
Bowl, mixing, 1½ qt., vertical pattern	55.00
Bowl, mixing, 2½ qt.	55.00
Bowl, mixing, 3½ qt.	65.00
Creamer	10.00
Cup, 5 oz., snack	5.00

	White w/decals
Cup, 8 oz.	7.50
Mug, 8 oz.	20.00
Plate, 7⅜", salad	14.00
Plate, 10" dinner	12.00
Platter, 9" x 12"	22.50
Saucer, 5¾"	2.50
Sugar	10.00
Sugar cover	5.00
Tray, 11" x 6", snack	8.00

Dinnerware & Patterns

BLUE MOSAIC 1966 – 1969

Colors: White w/decals

Blue Mosaic snack sets remain plentiful with many of these being found in the original boxes. Make sure the box is in beautiful condition if you are going to pay a premium for it. Right now, you can afford to wait for a better appearing one if you feel the price is too much. The snack tray in Blue Mosaic is oval and not rectangular as are most Fire-King patterns.

I have observed a few pieces of Blue Mosaic in Florida as I travel, but most have been found in central Ohio and western Pennsylvania. The Mosaic cup, creamer, and sugar do not have the Mosaic pattern on them and are a solid blue color matching the blue in the patterned design on the other pieces. That same blue cup resides upon both the snack tray and saucer. No patterned cups were made as far as I can determine.

The prices on most pieces of Blue Mosaic have remained steady except for **mint** condition bowls and plates. As with many decaled patterns, usage wear and tear on items is all too apparent. If you plan on using the dishes, you can be a bit more tolerant of condition than if you are collecting them with investment goals in mind.

Different areas of the country often seem to have an abundance of one pattern and a scarcity of others. Pricing for this book has resulted in many long telephone and Internet discussions about these regional differences. Commonly found pieces in Florida or Ohio may be rarely seen in Texas or vice versa; prices often reflect these fluctuations in availability making it hard for authors who try to find a common ground in pricing.

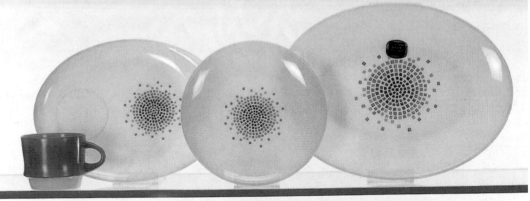

This short-lived Anchor Hocking pattern was shown only in a 1966 – 1967 catalog. Add $2.00 to $3.00 for an original label on any item. The boxes for snack sets run from $5.00 to $15.00 depending upon condition.

As the popularity of later made Fire-King patterns continues to grow, there will probably be more of it available at Depression glass shows. Some dealers and glass show committees still ignore these more recent patterns, but most are trying to keep up with the changing collecting market by stocking and allowing patterns to be shown that customers are asking for — no matter when it was manufactured! However, if you cannot locate your pattern at a local glass show, there is always the Internet.

	White w/decals
Bowl, 4⅝", dessert	8.00
Bowl, 6⅝", soup plate	14.00
Bowl, 8¼", vegetable	18.00
Creamer	8.00
Cup, 7½ oz.	4.00
Plate, 7⅜", salad	8.00
Plate, 10", dinner	9.00
Platter, 9" x 12"	17.50
Saucer, 5¾"	2.00
Sugar	8.00
Sugar cover	5.00
Tray, 10" x 7½", oval, snack	6.00

"BUBBLE" 1941 – 1968

Colors: Desert Gold, crystal, Forest Green, green, Iridescent, Jade-ite, Lustre, Sapphire blue, pink, Royal Ruby, Milk White, and fired-on Vitrock colors

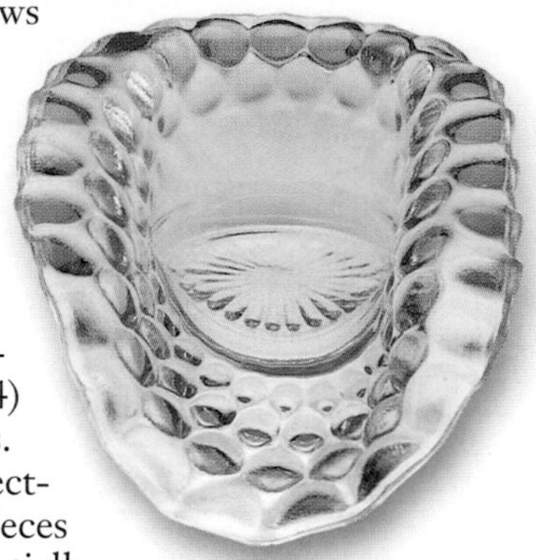

"Bubble" first appeared in the 1940 Anchor Hocking catalog with a designation of Bullseye. That first catalog listing is for the Rose 8⅜" bowl; but in 1941, that bowl and the 10" plate (with four rows of bubbles around the center) were introduced in crystal. Pink is now hard to find except for that omnipresent 8⅜" bowl. In 1972, when I first visited Anchor Hocking, there were stacks and stacks of these bowls sitting in a corner of one of their buildings. I have often wondered what happened to those.

"Bubble" is the one pattern easily recognized by beginning collectors. Too, the exceedingly simplified, orbicular bubbles have managed to be timeless in blending as well with today's decorating themes as they did when first issued.

The highly collected Sapphire blue ovenware was introduced in 1941, but Sapphire "Bubble" is not illustrated until a 1946 catalog. An 8" and a 4" bowl were pictured in a war era (1944) catalog, but these were only listed as crystal. Those two sizes were never again listed in catalogs.

Blue cups, saucers, and dinner plates are abundant and readily obtained. Nevertheless, collecting a complete set of "Bubble" is a different matter! **Basic** pieces are abundant in blue; other pieces are in much lesser supply. Creamers have always been scarce, but the 9" flanged bowl has essentially disappeared from the collecting domain. There are now two variations of this 9" bowl pictured on page 17! The flatter one was turned down a bit more than those previously seen; thus, it is not as deep. I might mention the blue whimsy and deep cereal here. A whimsy is a nonproduction piece that a factory worker made on his own. This one was made from a bowl and its intended use is a mystery, though a pipe holder has been mentioned. The cereal bowl is about a quarter inch deeper than those normally found. It could have been experimental.

Crystal "Bubble" is beginning to attract new admirers. However, the crystal "Bubble" pitcher continues to be their nemesis. That hammered aluminum piece (pg. 14) was designed around a dinner plate. I have seen several of these; so, it must have been a stock item for someone; but it was not an Anchor Hocking production item.

Three different lines of Anchor Hocking stems were sold with "Bubble." The Early American Line (pg. 14) is commonly called the "Bubble" stem. The Royal Ruby stem line shown on page 15 was named "Boopie" by another author, but was sold as Berwick and the Inspiration iced teas (swirled pattern on base) shown in the box at the bottom of page 17 were also called "Burple" by that same author. (I include those odd names so you will know what advertisers are talking about in their ads.) The Early American stemware can be found in crystal, Forest Green, and Royal Ruby. Berwick is found in those same colors plus amber. Inspiration tumblers can only be found in Forest Green. There are small, crystal plates available to match the Inspiration tumbler line.

Yellow and Peach Lustre "Bubble" bowls have attracted few collectors so far, but there is now a big demand for the Jade-ite bowl even though it is relatively plentiful. Jade-ite is the key word!

A 1946 ad guaranteed this Fire-King tableware to be "heat-proof," indeed a "tableware that can be used in the oven, on the table, in the refrigerator." This added magnitude is unique to Fire-King since most Depression glass patterns do not hold up to sudden changes in temperature. Forest Green or Royal Ruby "Bubble" do not profess these heat-proof capabilities, however; so be advised! Only Sapphire and crystal "Bubble" were issued as Fire-King, but Forest Green and Royal Ruby are as eagerly sought by collectors as are their earlier counterparts!

Forest Green (dark green) and Royal Ruby (red) dinner plates have both become difficult to find without scratches and knife marks on the surface. It's hard to believe that in the late 1970s a Georgia dealer found a warehouse filled with several thousand Royal Ruby dinner plates and over three hundred tidbit trays; and today, both are priced as hard to find! Many collectors use the red and green "Bubble" for their Christmas tables. Christmas has just passed as I write this, but since we were leaving the next morning, we succumbed to the colorful Christmas paper plate system this year in order to speed clean-up and have more quality time with the family.

The large, footed, green vase on page 16 has turned up in two other collections. I paid $35.00 for the one pictured, but one of the others was found for $15.00. They do not seem to be common.

The original labels on the crystal "Bubble" on page 14 read "Heat Proof." Add $1.00 to $2.00 to prices of crystal with labels and $2.00 to $3.00 for labels on blue. Only Forest Green or Royal Ruby labels are found on those colored pieces of "Bubble."

	Crystal Iridescent	Forest Green	Sapphire Blue	Royal Ruby	White
Bowl, 4", berry	4.00		17.50		
Bowl, 4½", fruit	4.50	11.00	15.00	8.00	4.50
Bowl, 5¼", cereal	10.00	20.00	15.00		
Bowl, 7¾", flat soup	12.00		15.00		15.00
Bowl, 8⅜", large berry	10.00	14.00	16.50	20.00	10.00

Dinnerware & Patterns

	Crystal Iridescent	Forest Green	Sapphire Blue	Royal Ruby	White
Bowl, 8½", shallow (pink $8.00; Jade-ite, Vitrock $16.00)					
Bowl, 9", flanged (2 styles)			395.00		
Candlesticks, pr.	16.00	37.50	45.00 (black)		
*Creamer	6.00	12.00	35.00		6.50
**Cup	3.50	7.00	5.00	8.00	5.00
Lamp, three styles	40.00				
Pitcher, 64 oz., ice lip	90.00			60.00	
Plate, 6¾", bread and butter	3.00	18.00			3.00
Plate, 9⅜", grill			22.50		
**Plate, 9⅜", dinner	7.00	25.00	7.00	24.00	9.00
Platter, 12", oval	15.00		16.00		
****Saucer	1.00	4.00	1.50	4.00	2.00
***Stem, 3½ oz., cocktail	4.00	14.00		10.00	
***Stem, 4 oz., juice	4.50	15.00		10.00	
Stem, 4½ oz., cocktail	4.00	12.50		12.50	
Stem, 5½ oz., juice	5.00	12.50		12.50	
***Stem, 6 oz., sherbet	3.00	9.00		7.00	
Stem, 6 oz., sherbet	3.50	9.00		9.00	
***Stem, 9 oz., goblet	7.00	15.00		12.50	
Stem, 9½ oz., goblet	7.00	13.00		13.00	
***Stem, 14 oz., iced tea	9.00	16.00			
Sugar	6.00	12.00	25.00		6.50
Tidbit, 2 tier				67.50	
Tumbler, 6 oz., juice	3.50			8.00	
Tumbler, 8 oz., 3¼", old fashioned	10.00			16.00	
Tumbler, 9 oz., water	5.00			9.00	
Tumbler, 12 oz., 4½", iced tea	12.00			12.50	
Tumbler, 16 oz., 5⅞", lemonade	14.00			16.00	

*Desert Gold – $25.00   **Pink – $125.00   ***Berwick or Inspiration   ****Pink – $40.00

"Bubble"

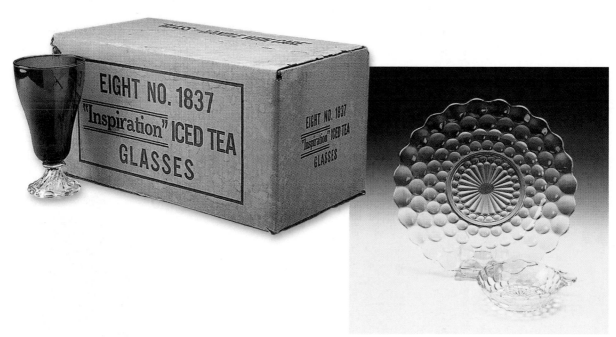

⚓ CHARM 1950 – 1956

Colors: Azur-ite, Forest Green, Ivory, Jade-ite, pink, Royal Ruby, Milk White

Anchor Hocking's Charm pattern was first introduced in Jade-ite and Azur-ite in the 1950 catalog. Charm dishes are square and were listed into 1954. Although Forest Green and Royal Ruby squared sets were shown side by side with Jade-ite and Azur-ite, at no time are those sets ever listed by any other name than Forest Green or Royal Ruby.

Jade-ite Charm is the color most collected and the color that has seen the greatest upsurge in price since the first book. Azur-ite is another Charm color that collectors seek, but only moderate gains in price have been made there. The Royal Ruby 7⅜" salad bowl has more than doubled in price and that one astounds me! I did not realize how hard they had become to find until a collector asked me to find her one. I found two in six months and they sold the first show where I displayed them after she balked at a price of $50.00. Six months later they are selling for $75.00. Only five pieces are found in Royal Ruby with that salad bowl becoming difficult. The one pictured in row 2 on page 19 was turned up to add height to the photo, making it look more like a plate!

Only the creamer and sugar have been found in Anchorwhite and many of those are trimmed in 22K gold as pictured on the bottom of page 19. A boxed set (pictured in the first edition of this book) originally sold for $2.59 according to a price sticker found on it. Forest Green dinners and soup bowls remain elusive, but platters are definitely off the endangered species list for now. Remember that these were used as everyday dishes; so, be aware of the use marks and scratches on these items. All prices listed are for **mint** condition items!

Pictured here are an Ivory luncheon plate and a cartoon Charm plate. These were sold as souvenir items and the red design was added outside of the Hocking factory. Ivory Charm is rarely seen; but only avid collectors pay much attention to any of the odd colored pieces in Charm.

The 8⅜" Charm plate is listed in the 1950 catalog as a dinner plate, but in all later catalogs as a luncheon plate. Subsequently, a 10" plate was listed for a while, but these only measure 9¼". Azur-ite and Jade-ite labels add $2.00 to $4.00 to the price; but, Forest Green, and Royal Ruby labels only add $.50 to $1.00 depending upon the piece. Only a few pieces of Charm are actually marked Fire-King; however, most collectors are more interested in the Charm dishes than they are in the marking.

	Azur-ite White	Forest Green	Jade-ite Ivory	Royal Ruby
Bowl, 4¾", dessert	6.00	8.00	14.00	8.00
Bowl, 6", soup	15.00	20.00	35.00	
Bowl, 7⅜", salad	17.50	18.00	60.00	75.00
Creamer	12.00	7.50	20.00	
Cup	4.00	5.00	**12.00	6.00
Plate, 6⅝", salad	9.00	10.00	40.00	
Plate, 8⅜", luncheon	8.50	8.00	**25.00	10.00
Plate, 9¼", dinner	22.00	30.00	45.00	
Platter, 11" x 8"	25.00	22.00	55.00	
* Saucer, 5⅜"	1.50	1.50	**5.00	2.50
Sugar	12.00	7.50	20.00	

*Pink – $20.00

** Ivory

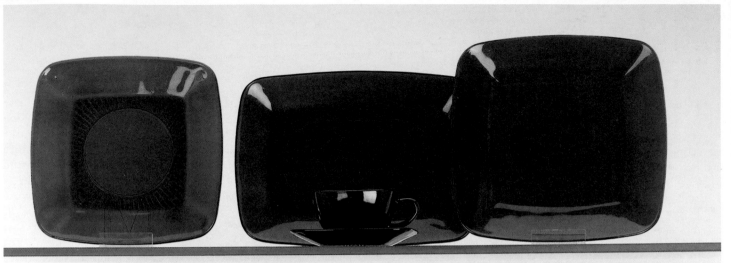

CLASSIC, "RACHAEL" 1963 – 1972

Colors: Crystal, Milk White w/22K gold, Royal Ruby

I included this smaller Fire-King pattern because there seems to be some serious confusion between it and Golden Shell. I have received numerous letters with pictures of the snack set asking why I did not have it photographed and listed under Golden Shell. The major reason was that it was not Golden Shell. I have pictured a snack set in the box so you will see the proper name for this snack set.

I have seen some of the snack cups with Golden Shell stickers. I do not know if they were factory applied or someone added the stickers later. Those who collect items with labels need to be careful about that. Many Jade-ite labels were on all kinds of pieces and can be reapplied to other items to increase the value. It's been done for years with Cambridge, Heisey, and Fostoria. Many times labels have been mistakenly applied to pieces that were not of that company's manufacture. What makes you think that Fire-King would be immune to unscrupulous people? I even received some Fire-King pieces represented as mint condition because they had labels. It had labels, but was worn from years of use. The Internet auctions have brought out all kinds of sellers and it is not always as safe to buy there as from established dealers. Unfortunately, I'm beginning to hear more reports of this ilk. Perhaps you should inquire about the "return" policies of these dealers. Buyers beware!

The Royal Ruby 10" vase, the 5" and 11" bowls, and 14" plate are all sought by Royal Ruby collectors. Sometimes you can find these items with the Royal Ruby sticker still attached. Crystal is rarely found, but that scarcity is seldom realized since so few collectors are presently seeking it. If you wish a challenge, try to find crystal pieces of Classic.

	Crystal	Royal Ruby	White
Bowl, 5¼", deep	6.00		7.50
Bowl, 11", deep	25.00	55.00	22.50
Bowl, 12", oval			15.00
Chip & Dip, 5½" w/11" bowls	35.00		35.00
Cup, snack, 5 oz.	3.00		3.00
Plate, 10¾" x 6½" snack	5.00		7.00
Plate, 14½"	17.50	35.00	22.50
Vase, 10"		65.00	

Dinnerware & Patterns

Colors: Crystal, Laser Blue, Royal Ruby, Honey Gold, and tints

Dinnerware & Patterns

Repeating information from the first book for new readers, Early American Prescut is usually abbreviated EAPC; to save space, I will do the same. With four pieces, EAPC was introduced by Anchor Hocking in the 1960 – 1961 catalog. Most pieces were discontinued by 1978, except for the creamer, sugar, cruet, and shakers with plastic tops which were made as late as 1997. The only piece currently listed is the 8½" vase which is being sold to the florist industry. Many items were only made for a year or two, resulting in a smaller supply than the collecting public is used to seeing. Some collectors have dubbed this pattern "Star of David."

I have spent three years studying the collecting whims of EAPC collectors. I deliberately pursued the harder to find items. There are some scarce items besides the cocktail shaker, bud vase, and 3½" footed sherbet which may have been experimental or nonproduction items.

I have found the four-part 11" plate or relish with swirled dividers to be the hardest to find piece of the regular production. The reason may be pictured on page 26. It seems these were sent to Taiwan and made into a lazy Susan by adding a wooden base. These were then shipped back for sale here. Some never made the trip back or are still in use by non-collectors. The next group of items equally difficult to find are the 11¾" paneled bowl, 6¾" plates with or without the cup ring, 5¼" bowl (1¼" deep), and the oil lamp with glass threads for burner. The next tier of difficulty is the oil lamp with brass insert for the burner, individual shakers, 13½", five-part relish, lamp shades, and possibly **mint** condition iced teas.

The two styles of oil lamps are pictured side by side on page 27. Also notice the openings that vary greatly on the square pitchers shown on page 27. The one with the smaller opening will hold 48 ounces instead of the 40 ounces listed in factory catalogs. There are a few minor variations in other pieces, but these are the major ones. Time will tell if prices will vary on the different styles.

Punch bowl sets still abound as do cruets, regular shakers, creamers, sugars, gondola bowls, and most of the items priced less than $10.00. Cathy was recently startled to see her hair stylist using a 4¼" EAPC bowl to hold streaking bleach.

The 5¼" bowl (1¼" deep) can easily be found in Avocado green (page 27) but is rarely seen in crystal. Colored EAPC is in higher demand if it is not flashed-on color (top page 28). Laser blue ($50.00) and Honey Gold ($35.00) sugar and lids shown on page 27 are the more desirable pieces. Quantities of Royal Ruby 7¾" ashtrays have turned up and the price has decreased on these since the previous book. The three colored vases on page 27 are somewhat controversial. They are Anchor Hocking, but they have horizontal ribs up the side that do not occur on other EAPC items. They sell for $25.00 to $35.00, if you wish to add some color to your collection.

Remember that the two sizes of powder jars (4" and 5") are not strictly EAPC. They are marked **Italy** around the star in the center. There is a heart shaped box as well as a small, divided bowl that you will find marked Italy, too.

The items without the star are another pattern simply called Prescut which can be found on page 29. All pieces in the EAPC list have the star except the cup and the double candle. The catalog depiction on the bottom of page 28 shows the star on the top where you will find a knob today. In talking to some mould makers for Hocking, I was told there were many battles from design conception to actual working mould. Sometimes the design was unable to be carried out and still remove the piece from the mould. Evidently, this was one of those pieces.

There are a multitude of tidbit and relish trays using all sorts of EAPC pieces. A couple of these are shown on the top of page 25. None are factory assembled, but many collectors like to add them to their sets. Most can be found in the $15.00 to $20.00 range.

Boxes add $10.00 – 25.00 to the price depending upon size and condition. A punch set in a box is more desirable than a boxed creamer and sugar for example. I got a chuckle from a guy fussing about paying "extra" for an ugly box on the Internet when all he wanted was the glass! A Texas collector has found items which say "Made in Mexico."

	Crystal		Crystal
Ashtray, 4", #700/690	5.00	Bowl, 9", oval, #776	7.00
Ashtray, 5"	10.00	Bowl, 9⅜", gondola dish, #752	4.00
* Ashtray, 7¾", #718-G	15.00	Bowl, 10¾", salad, #788	12.00
Bowl, 4¼", #726 (scalloped rim)	7.00	Bowl, 11¾", paneled, #794	225.00
Bowl, 4¼", #726 (smooth rim)	20.00	Butter, bottom w/metal handle and knife	15.00
Bowl, 5¼" (1¼" deep)	35.00	Butter, w/cover, ¼ lb., #705	6.00
Bowl, 5¼", #775 (scalloped rim)	7.00	Cake plate, 13½", ftd., #706	32.50
Bowl, 5¾", dessert, #765	2.50	Candlestick, 7" x 5⅝", double, #784	32.00
Bowl, 6¾", three-toed, #768	4.50	Candy, w/lid, 5¼", #774	10.00
Bowl, 7¼", round, #767	6.00	Candy, w/cover, 7¼" x 5½", #792	12.00
Bowl, 7¼", (scalloped rim)	20.00	Chip & dip, 10¾" bowl, 5¼",	
Bowl, 8¾", #787	9.00	brass finish holder, #700/733	27.50
Bowl, 9", console, #797	15.00	Coaster, #700/702	2.00

	Crystal
Cocktail shaker, 9", 30 oz.	495.00
Creamer, #754	3.00
Cruet, w/stopper, 7¾", #711	6.00
Cup, punch or snack, 6 oz. (no star)	2.50
Lazy Susan, 9 pc., #700/713	45.00
Oil lamp	325.00
Pitcher, 18 oz., #744	8.00
Pitcher, 40 to 48 oz., square (2 styles)	55.00
Pitcher, 60 oz., #791	15.00
Plate, 6¾"	55.00
Plate, 6¾", w/ring for 6 oz. cup	50.00
Plate, 10", snack, #780	10.00
Plate, 11", 4-part w/swirl dividers	150.00
Plate, 11"	12.00
Plate, 11¾", deviled egg/relish, #750	42.00
Plate, 13½", serving, #790	12.50
Punch set, 15 pc.	33.00
Relish, 8½", oval, 3-part, #778	5.00
Relish, 10", divided, tab hdld., #770	7.00

	Crystal
Relish, 11⅞", 3-part, rectangular	25.00
Relish, 13½", five part	28.00
Server, 12 oz. (syrup), #707	20.00
Shakers, pr., metal tops, #700/699	6.00
Shakers, pr., plastic tops, #725	5.00
Shakers, pr., 2¼" individual, #700/736	75.00
Sherbet, 3½", 6 oz., ftd.	350.00
Sugar, w/lid, #753	4.00
Tray, 6½" x 12", hostess, #750	12.50
Tray, cr/sug, #700/671	3.00
Tumbler, 5 oz., 4", juice, #730	5.00
Tumbler, 10 oz., 4½" tumbler, #731	4.00
Tumbler, 15 oz., 6" tumbler, #732	20.00
Vase, 5", ftd., vase	500.00
Vase, 6" x 4½", basket/block, #704/205	18.00
Vase, 8½", #741	8.00
Vase, 10", #742	12.50

*Royal Ruby – $25.00

Dinnerware & Patterns

EARLY AMERICAN PRESCUT

	PACKING
796—11¾ x 11¾" Deviled Egg & Relish Tray	½ doz. — 20 lbs.
700/671— 4 Pce. Sugar and Creamer Set	6 sets — 16 lbs.
(6 Sets Bulk Packed in 1 Carton)	
Consists of one Sugar & Cover, one Creamer and one Tray	

770—10" Divided Relish Dish	1 doz. — 18 lbs.
784— 7 x 5⅝" Twin Candelabra	1 doz. — 20 lbs.

PRESCUT: "OATMEAL" & "PINEAPPLE," 1941 – 1970s

There has been confusion among collectors as to what constitutes EAPC and what does not. All EAPC items were designated by Anchor Hocking as line number 700. "Oatmeal" Prescut pieces are similar to EAPC pieces, but without the "star." The
"Oatmeal" name comes from the fact that seven of these pieces were premiums in boxes of Crystal Wedding Oats. These items,
as well as the cigarette or jewel box, have line numbers in the 500s or 600s. The soap dish may not have been in the oatmeal
boxes, but it is the same pattern. You can tell by its price that it is not as common as the others. Like the five pieces of Forest
Green Sandwich that were packed in oatmeal, these items are abundant today. All three sizes of Prescut tumblers have concave
sides whereas EAPC tumblers are straight sided. If you wish to collect these with EAPC, go ahead; do not pay a big price for
these being touted as EAPC. They are simply Prescut, not EAPC. The 6" and 9" bud vases (first listed, 1949) are often represented as Early American Prescut, but are Prescut only with line numbers 1070 and 1071. See page 115.

The other pattern often mistakenly identified as EAPC has been called "Pineapple" by collectors. It was first shown in the
1941 catalog, twenty years before the birth of EAPC. This can be found mostly in crystal with an occasional piece in white. You
might even find white items decorated with painted flowers. For an exciting decoration on this white, turn to page 222. The
crystal cigarette box and marmalade can both be found with a Royal Ruby lid. This adds to their value since Royal Ruby collectors also want these pieces for their collections.

"OATMEAL"

	Crystal
Bowl, 4¼", berry	2.00
Cup	2.50
Saucer, 4⅜"	1.50
Sherbet, 5 oz.	1.50
Soap dish, 5¼" x 3¾"	18.00
Tumbler, 4 oz., juice	2.00
Tumbler, 7 oz., old fashioned	2.50
Tumbler, 9 oz., water	2.00

"PINEAPPLE"

	Crystal	White
Box, 4¾", cigarette or dresser	15.00	12.50
Box, 4¾", w/Royal Ruby lid	25.00	
Butter, round	15.00	
* Marmalade, w/Royal Ruby lid	18.00	
Pitcher, 12 oz., milk	8.00	10.00
Salt and Pepper, pr.	12.00	
* Sugar w/lid, handled	10.00	12.00
Sugar w/lid, no handles	10.00	
Syrup pitcher	12.00	
Tumbler, 10 oz., iced tea	6.00	8.00

*add 50% for painted flowers

FIRE-KING DINNERWARE "PHILBE" 1937 – 1938

Colors: blue, green, pink, and crystal

Fire-King dinnerware is the bane of many collectors of both Fire-King and Depression glass. Those who try to find one piece or color of each pattern end up searching in vain for "Philbe." Fire-King dinnerware is often their "last" pattern to find. It is rarely seen and with each passing year, fewer and fewer pieces are being discovered. For pieces of Fire-King Dinnerware to come into the marketplace now, there almost has to be a long-time collection sold.

I found only four pieces last year and three of those were happened upon the morning I left for the photography session for this book. One of those wound up with a collector who came to help me photograph. I have a hard time keeping this pattern when helpful collectors start begging with tears to let them buy just one piece! If you want a piece for your collection, do not hesitate in buying it when you find some for sale! Even if you do not want to keep it, someone will gladly take it off your hands!

Green grill plates or luncheon plates might end up in your collection with more ease than anything else in Fire-King dinnerware. For now, any color 6" saucer/sherbet plate is rarer than the aforementioned plates. Cups are nigh impossible to find!

I have a stack of Fire-King dinnerware individual photos that have been used in my books over the years, but attaining enough for a large group setting is becoming extremely difficult! You can see additional pieces pictured in my *Very Rare Glassware of the Depression Years, Second Series*, including the blue candy dish, tall water goblet, and green cookie jar. Over the last few years, a few 4¾" sherbets have finally surfaced — five green and two blue to be exact! You can see one of the blue ones pictured at the bottom of page 31.

I still need a green candy lid if anyone should run into one in their travels. The only green lid to surface was for a green cookie jar. They are so similar in size (like Cameo) that even knowledgeable dealers often confuse them.

Blue pieces often have an added platinum trim as can be seen in the photograph. Most of the platinum banded, blue pieces known turned up in 1975 or reside in Anchor Hocking's morgue. I have yet to see blue Mayfair trimmed in platinum. This seems strange since these patterns were contemporaries. The infrequently found blue items include footed tumblers of which the tea is found more often than the water. That is why the water is priced higher than the tea in this particular pattern.

Only the oval vegetable bowl is periodically found in pink although you could not prove it by my pictures. That oval bowl is also available in green and crystal (pictured).

On my first trip to Anchor Hocking in June 1972, there was a large set of "Philbe" in a window display in the showroom. Then, all I knew was that it had the same shape as Cameo and the color of blue Mayfair. I noted that the footed tumblers and goblets had the Mayfair shape. Unfortunately, few pieces seem to have been retained for the morgue today.

This pattern was named "Philbe" by another author in honor of a Mr. Philip Bee who worked at Anchor Hocking and helped authors working on preserving the history of that company's glass.

	Crystal	Pink, Green	Blue
Bowl, 5½", cereal	18.00	45.00	65.00
Bowl, 7¼", salad	50.00	80.00	115.00
Bowl, 10", oval vegetable	60.00	90.00	165.00
Candy jar, 4", low, with cover	215.00	725.00	795.00
Cookie jar with cover	600.00	950.00	1,500.00
Creamer, 3¼", ftd.	70.00	135.00	150.00
Cup	55.00	110.00	175.00
Goblet, 7¼", 9 oz., thin	75.00	185.00	235.00
Pitcher, 6", 36 oz., juice	295.00	625.00	895.00
Pitcher, 8½", 56 oz.	395.00	925.00	1,175.00
Plate, 6", sherbet	40.00	65.00	95.00
Plate, 8", luncheon	20.00	37.50	47.50
Plate, 10", heavy sandwich	32.50	75.00	100.00
Plate, 10½", salver	40.00	75.00	90.00
Plate, 10½", grill	40.00	75.00	95.00
Plate, 11⅝", salver	22.50	62.50	95.00
Platter, 12", closed handles	30.00	125.00	175.00
Saucer, 6" (same as sherbet plate)	40.00	65.00	95.00

	Crystal	Pink, Green	Blue
Sherbet, 3¾"	75.00		
Sherbet, 4¾"		450.00	550.00
Sugar, 3¼" ftd.	70.00	135.00	150.00
Tumbler, 4", 9 oz., flat water	40.00	105.00	130.00
Tumbler, 3½", ftd. juice	40.00	150.00	175.00
Tumbler, 5¼", 10 oz., ftd.	40.00	80.00	100.00
Tumbler, 6½", 15 oz., ftd. iced tea	50.00	85.00	90.00

Dinnerware & Patterns

31

"FISH SCALE" 1939 – 1943, 1963 – 1965

Colors: Crystal, Lustre, Vitrock, Victrock w/blue or red trim

Anchor Hocking's catalogs list this as Ivory Glass Tableware, but the collectors' name "Fish Scale" seems more descriptive for this smaller pattern. *All catalog references and listings of Ivory refer to what we call Vitrock today and was what Anchor Hocking most often called it!*

This Ivory Glass Tableware was produced as plain Ivory, Decorated, and Red Band. The Decorated is illustrated by the pieces in blue and red with the **wide** color band on the edge and the Red Band is shown by those items with a **narrow** band on the inside of the piece. There has been little price differentiation between Red Band and Decorated. There will have to be more collectors seeking "Fish Scale" to determine whether there will be pricing divisions. Prices for all blue items and some red have increased. The biggest hike has been in the platter that is turning out to be rare.

The picture at the bottom of this page shows items missing from the first edition photo. The crystal bowl is the only crystal item being found with any regularity.

Blue pieces were never listed in any Anchor Hocking catalogs that I have seen; so, blue does not seem to be as available as the red decorated or trimmed pieces. Evidently, the blue was a special order item and not a standard, stocked pattern.

The Ivory demitasse cup and saucer pictured on page 33 are from the morgue, but a few have been found for sale according-ing to collectors searching for them.

	Ivory	Ivory w/blue	Ivory w/red
Bowl, 5½", dessert, shallow	10.00		15.00
Bowl, 5½", cereal, deep	12.00		18.00
Bowl, 7½", soup	18.00		30.00
* Bowl, 8¾", vegetable	30.00		35.00
** Cup, demitasse	35.00		
Cup, 8 oz.	8.00	25.00	10.00
Plate, 7⅜", salad	8.00		15.00
Plate, 9¼", dinner	13.00	35.00	20.00
Platter, 11¾	45.00	60.00	65.00
*** Saucer, demitasse	25.00		
Saucer	3.00	8.00	4.00

*Crystal - $20.00   ** Lustre – $10.00   *** Lustre – $12.50

Dinnerware & Patterns

FLEURETTE 1958 – 1961

Fleurette first appeared in Anchor Hocking's 1959 – 1960 catalog printed in April 1958. The 1960 – 1961 catalog is the last time it appears; so Fleurette was made for a much shorter time than the Primrose pattern that followed. I see sets of Fleurette when out on buying trips rather than a piece here and there.

One major concern for collectors is that this floral decoration is susceptible to wear; many of the sets I have seen offered for sale have flowers totally missing or obscured.

Several noteworthy pieces include the mug, egg plate, Lace Edge 13" plate, and 4⅛", 9½ ounce water tumbler. Few of these have ever been seen! Chili bowls and bread and butter and salad plates are seen infrequently; and soup bowls are a bane for many collectors.

Basic pieces were sold in large sets and are commonly found today. The first book showed catalog pages listing these larger sets if you would like to check their make-up. So far, Fleurette has not had the surge of collectors buying it as do other Fire-King patterns; therefore, if you are searching for a pattern where prices are fairly reasonable, take a look at Fleurette. Just remember to buy mint condition pieces — if you're buying for possible resale at some future time. If you're planning to use this durable ware daily, lesser condition pieces should be available at 25% to 75% less than listed, depending upon how worn the decals are.

Dinnerware & Patterns

	White w/decals
Bowl, 4⅝", dessert	3.00
Bowl, 5", chili	20.00
Bowl, 6⅝", soup plate	12.00
Bowl, 8¼", vegetable	11.00
Creamer	5.00
Cup, 5 oz., snack	3.00
Cup, 8 oz.	4.00
Egg plate	150.00
Plate, 6¼", bread and butter	14.00
Plate, 7⅜", salad	10.00
Plate, 9⅛", dinner	5.00

	White w/decals
Plate, 13" (Lace Edge)	125.00
Platter, 9" x 12"	14.00
Mug	75.00
Saucer, 5¾"	1.00
Sugar	5.00
Sugar cover	5.00
Tumbler, 4⅛", 9½ oz., water	95.00
Tray, 11" x 6", snack	4.00

FOREST GREEN 1950 – 1965

Forest Green was a **color** made by Anchor Hocking and not a pattern per se. Forest Green color was utilized for the square Charm blank (1950), and subsequently, that glassware became better known by its color identification. Even Anchor Hocking's "Bubble" was christened Forest Green dinnerware. You will find many odd, dark green pieces on the market that look like Forest Green. To actually be Forest Green, it must have been manufactured by Anchor Hocking! Although there were several hundred pieces made in Forest Green, all the basic pieces are cataloged here.

You may recognize that the stems priced here are also priced under "Bubble" on page 12. An explanation of the three stemware lines is also there. Numerous collectors use the Forest Green Anchor Hocking stems to go with "Bubble," Forest Green, or even some china patterns.

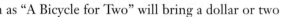

The ashtray pictured on the cover and at the bottom of page 38 was given to me by a former mould maker. He told me that only a few were made, and the design was never incorporated into Anchor Hocking's line. It seems unusual to spend the money to make a mould and not use it, but it obviously happened.

The boxed sets of tumblers on page 38 will sell for $5.00 – 8.00 more than the price of the six tumblers themselves. You can add an additional $1.00 for Forest Green labels. Labels are fairly common, but Fire-King collectors have become excited about them. Notice the 9 ounce tumblers on the fourth row of that page. The metal caps were covers for dairy products such as cottage cheese. In my former Kentucky area, it was Sealtest brand dairy products. Some tumblers were packed with apple jelly and others with honey. It was great advertising for Anchor Hocking and good for the retailer and the consumer. Decorated tumblers such as "A Bicycle for Two" will bring a dollar or two more than regular tumblers when they sell. Plain tumblers sell more frequently.

On page 39 is a relish set using a Forest Green Waterford plate as a base. It is pictured with the original box. I have placed the **center** piece of that relish next to a sherbet so you can see the difference in those two items. The three pint water bottle with screw-on top which is generally only found in crystal, is quite rare in Forest Green. Hand-painted vases have caught the eye of some collectors and that is driving up the price of those being found. Oft times, these are souvenir pieces with scenes from well-known places such as Niagara Falls.

Forest Green punch bowl sets sell especially well around Christmas. The punch bowls themselves were sold along with eight of the 5¼" deep bowls as popcorn sets. That is why punch bowl bases are harder to find than the bowls and sell for as much as the bowls themselves.

Ashtray, 3½", square	5.00	** Stem, 9½ oz., goblet	13.00
Ashtray, 4⅝", square	6.00	* Stem, 14 oz., iced tea	14.00
Ashtray, 5¾", square	9.00	Tumbler, 5 oz., 3½"	4.00
Ashtray, 5¾", hexagonal	8.00	Tumbler, 7 oz.	4.00
Batter bowl w/spout	28.00	Tumbler, 9 oz, table	5.00
Bowl, 4¾", dessert	5.50	Tumbler, 9 oz., fancy	6.00
Bowl, 5¼", deep	8.50	Tumbler, 9½ oz., tall	6.50
Bowl, 6", mixing	9.00	Tumbler, 10 oz., ftd., 4½"	6.50
Bowl, 8½", oval vegetable	21.00	Tumbler, 11 oz.	7.00
Cocktail shaker, 32 oz.	30.00	Tumbler, 13 oz., iced tea	7.50
Comport, 6½"	35.00	Tumbler, 14 oz., 5"	7.50
Pitcher, 22 oz.	22.50	Tumbler, 15 oz., long boy	11.00
Pitcher, 36 oz.	25.00	Tumbler, 15 oz., tall iced tea	17.00
Pitcher, 86 oz., round	40.00	Tumbler, 32 oz, giant iced tea	22.00
Plate, 6¾", salad	5.00	Vase, 3¾", several styles	6.00
Punch bowl	22.50	Vase, 4", ivy ball	5.00
Punch bowl stand	22.50	*** Vase, 6⅜"	6.00
Punch cup (round)	2.25	Vase, 6½"	6.00
Relish insert	6.00	Vase, 7"	8.00
Saucer, 5⅜"	1.50	Vase, 9"	12.00
Sherbet, flat	10.00	Vase, 9", bud	10.00
* Stem, 3½ oz., cocktail	10.00	Water bottle, w/glass lid	85.00
* Stem, 4 oz., juice	10.00	Water bottle, w/screw-on lid	125.00
** Stem, 4½ oz., cocktail	12.50		
** Stem, 5½ oz., juice	12.50	* Berwick or Inspiration	
** Stem, 6 oz., sherbet	9.00	** Early American Line	
* Stem, 6 oz., sherbet	6.00	*** Fired-on green – $9.00; cut – $20.00	
* Stem, 9 oz., goblet	10.00		

"FORGET ME NOT" "BLUE AND GOLD FLORAL" 1964 – 1966

Colors: White w/decal

"Forget Me Not" sugar bowls do exist! I have had several dozen pictures sent from collectors throughout the country. I even found one in a mall in Tampa. I was amazed that in that circle of Fire-King collectors and dealers who helped me on my first book, no one had ever seen a sugar. There were six or seven at the photography session this time and we seriously considered a photo of all of them for comic relief!

Apparently there were no Anchor Hocking catalog listings for "Forget Me Not"; so the only information available is from collectors who have pieces. The flower depicted appears to be a forget me not and the only colors known are blue and yellow. No boxed sets or labeled pieces have yet been found to solve the mystery of the real name.

My prediction in the first edition that all indications pointed to an ovenware line existing in "Forget Me Not" has come to fruition. Round and oval casseroles as well as a loaf pan and custard have emerged.

If you have, or find, pieces not listed, please let me know. A picture for confirmation would be helpful. Take the piece to be photographed outside on a bright, cloudy day and forget that the camera has a flash attachment. More photographs than you can imagine have been sent to me with the following disclaimer: "I know you cannot see this but…." If you can't see it and know what it really looks like, I guarantee that I will not be able to either!

	White w/decals		White w/decals
Bowl, 4⅝", dessert	8.00	Custard	8.00
Bowl, 5", chili or cereal	12.00	Loaf pan	25.00
Bowl, 6⅝", soup plate	18.00	Mug, 8 oz.	15.00
Bowl, 8¼", vegetable	20.00	Plate, 10", dinner	14.00
Casserole, 1 qt., w/cover	24.00	Platter, 9" x 12"	20.00
Casserole, 1½ qt., oval, w/cover	24.00	Sugar	12.00
Creamer	10.00	Sugar lid	5.00
Cup, 8 oz.	7.50	Saucer, 5¾"	2.50

Dinnerware & Patterns

GAME BIRDS 1959 – 1962

Colors: White w/decals

Anchor Hocking called these both Wild Birds and Game Birds, but the Game Birds seemed more apropos when I was considering an appellation for the first *Collectible Glassware from the 40s, 50s, 60s.* Today, Wild Birds might better characterize the evasiveness of some of the pieces.

Four birds are portrayed: Canadian goose, ringed-necked pheasant, ruffled grouse, and mallard duck. I only have catalog sheets of mugs, cereals, and ashtrays listed for 1960 – 1961; but as you can see on page 42, there are many more pieces available than those.

The only bird illustrated on any of the serving pieces is the ringed-neck pheasant. The sugar, creamer, 8¼" vegetable, and platter have only been discovered with that bird. Otherwise, items seem to be equally distributed among the four birds.

Price advances for the platter and vegetable bowls have been dramatic. The juice tumblers do not seem to be turning up regularly and the newly discovered 4⅛", 9½ ounce water tumbler with a ringed-neck pheasant is not turning up at all. A sudden abundance of 6¼" plates has dropped the price on that one item. Maybe a large supply of serving pieces will turn up in a warehouse somewhere. Don't laugh. Nearly every book I have written has had a story of some large supply of something surfacing in an attic, garage, or warehouse.

The largest distribution of Game Birds continues to be southwestern Missouri and Oklahoma. For some unknown reason, be it promotional sales or give-aways, this area is supplied with Game Birds. However, that abundance consists mostly of mugs, iced teas, cups, saucers, and plates. None of the hard-to-find pieces seem to have "flocked" there.

Many collectors use the mugs, bowls, and tumblers regularly. Those items will someday be in shorter supply because of this trend. Unhappily, there are not enough of these to supply everyone.

Men seem happier hunting for this pattern than others even if they are non-collectors and only helping a wife or friend. One woman told me she chose this pattern for their get-away cabin and her husband had really enjoyed both the hunt for the dishes and the use of them there.

	White w/decals
Ashtray, 5¼"	18.00
Bowl, 4⅝", dessert	5.00
Bowl, 5", chili or cereal	8.00
Bowl, 8¼", vegetable	60.00
Creamer	20.00
Mug, 8 oz.	8.00
Plate, 6¼", bread & butter	10.00
Plate, 9⅛", dinner	6.50
Platter, 12" x 9"	50.00
Sugar	20.00
Sugar cover	5.00
Tumbler, 5 oz., juice	35.00
Tumbler, 4⅛", 9½ oz., water	100.00
Tumbler, 11 oz., iced tea	12.00

Dinnerware & Patterns

41

HARVEST 1968 – 1971

Colors: White w/decals

The Harvest pattern has not yet reaped abundant devotees. However, enough do collect this limited pattern to pinpoint that the 7⅜" salad plate may be the most difficult piece to uncover. I was unable to scour one up for our photo shoot; if you have one, let me know.

I have found more collectors at least know what Harvest looks like than they did a couple of years ago. Advanced Jade-ite collectors have not paid much attention to the decaled patterns. They started with the older patterns and Jade-ite and are continuing their search for the more difficult pieces in those lines. A few older collectors of Fire-King actually look askance at the later patterns (the way some glass dealers do when Fire-King is mentioned). Don't be swayed by those attitudes if a pattern appeals to you!

Unfortunately, bowls have been arranged on their sides to show the pattern that is in the bottom of pieces. Harvest is found on Anchor Hocking's 4600 blank which has a stacking creamer, sugar, and cups, as does Blue Mosaic and Homestead.

Market accessibility to Harvest seems rather limited despite being in Anchor Hocking's catalogs for four years. That could mean that it is still being utilized by those people who bought it the late 1960s, or it has been packed away and people have yet to decide to sell it.

	White w/decals
Bowl, 4⅝", dessert	5.00
Bowl, 6⅝", soup plate	8.00
Bowl, 8¼", vegetable	15.00
Creamer	7.00
Cup, 7½ oz.	4.00
Plate, 7⅜", salad	10.00
Plate, 10", dinner	6.00
Platter, 9" x 12"	15.00
Saucer, 5¾"	2.00
Sugar	7.00
Sugar cover	5.00

HOBNAIL 1959 – 1979

Colors: Milk White and fired-on coral, green, and yellow

Dinnerware & Patterns

Hobnail is the first non-dinnerware pattern displayed in this book, but it is one pattern that some collectors are seeking because of its Milk White color. Also, Hobnail is being mixed with some other patterns that do not have beverage items, especially pitchers. Note the boxed water set. Rarely has this pattern been found boxed. In the past, the box was the first thing to go once a set had been opened.

I prefer the fired-on colors; but they seem to occur only on the vases and jardinieres.

The vertical column of horizontal ribs on all pieces of this Anchor Hocking Hobnail pattern distinguishes it from other companies' Hobnail patterns. That ribbing is very apparent on the tall vases in the photo.

Do not confuse this with the Hobnail that Anchor Hocking made in the 1930s and 1940s. (See *Collector's Encyclopedia of Depression Glass*.) There was no vertical column of ribs on that older pattern. If you find Ivory pieces such as the three-part cloverleaf or two-handled bowl, you have encountered Hocking's earlier Hobnail pattern. Those commonly found Ivory pieces have never been seen in Milk White. That older Hobnail design was also used on the very popular Moonstone pattern that was a mainstay of Anchor Hocking's during WW2.

Anchor Hocking always has had a great relationship with the florist trade and I suspect that many of these pieces of Hobnail were obtained with floral arrangements, much like the Soreno vases of the 1960s and Early American Prescut vases, today.

	Coral/Green/Yellow	Milk White
Cookie jar w/lid		25.00
Goblet, 13 oz., tea		6.00
Goblet, 9 oz., water		5.00
Jardiniere, 4½"	10.00	4.00
Jardiniere, 5½"	12.00	5.00
Pitcher, 18 oz.		12.50
Pitcher, 72 oz.		18.00
Tumbler, 9 oz., water		4.00
Vase, 9½"	*20.00	10.00

* Turquoise – $25.00

HOMESTEAD 1968 – 1971

Colors: White w/decals

Homestead is one of the decaled patterns I really like. It was introduced in the 1968 catalog on the 4600 line with stacking cup, creamer, and sugar, as was Harvest. Homestead appeared in catalogs for a year less than did Harvest; so, it should be in even shorter supply. Nonetheless, I have found more dealers familiar with Homestead than with Harvest. Maybe this pattern is finding favor with more collectors and/or dealer buyers. On the other hand, at least one collector stated that she found the pattern way too busy for her tastes. The intricate design is what intrigues me.

Kitchen items depicted are bounteous. There is a pepper and coffee grinder, coffee pot, cup and saucer, a teapot, a clock, an egg timer, a flower pot, and flower, basil, and clove containers, as well as other items; but you get the idea. Some artist had fun laying out this pattern; and today, some collectors are still enjoying his or her work.

If you wish to add this to your collection, begin immediately. Believe me, Fire-King patterns are disappearing from the market more rapidly than you would believe.

	White w/decals
Bowl, 4⅝", dessert	5.00
Bowl, 6⅝", soup plate	10.00
Bowl, 8¼", vegetable	18.00
Creamer	5.00
Cup, 7½ oz.	5.00
Plate, 7⅜", salad	15.00
Plate, 10", dinner	8.00
Platter, 9" x 12"	18.00
Saucer, 5¾"	2.00
Sugar	5.00
Sugar cover	5.00

HONEYSUCKLE 1959 – 1962

Colors: White w/decals

I see very little Honeysuckle in my constant travels about the country visiting malls and shops. Too, very little is being displayed at glass shows; so, accumulating a collection of Honeysuckle may be more difficult than I thought. Those Honeysuckle pieces that I have encountered have had strong designs still, unlike other patterns with decals. These decals seem to have held up better.

There are different **sizes** of decals being found. The soup bowls at each end of the lower row illustrate these size differences. The larger design is preferred by collectors, but it seems to be more scarce.

Three sizes of the rarely seen Honeysuckle tumblers are pictured, but the most unusual piece is the 9¾", three-part relish in the top row. The small berry bowl and 6¼" bread and butter plates are also being found irregularly. Boxed sets are difficult to find although a 53-piece boxed set is shown. Note that the box has Honeysuckle as two words. Evidently, the art department had no dictionary handy.

	White w/decals		White w/decals
Bowl, 4⅝", dessert	4.00	Platter, 9" x 12"	16.00
Bowl, 6⅝", soup plate	9.00	Relish, 9¾" three-part	100.00
Bowl, 8¼", vegetable	15.00	Saucer, 5¾"	1.50
Creamer	5.00	Sugar	5.00
Cup, 8 oz.	4.00	Sugar cover	5.00
Plate, 6¼", bread and butter	15.00	Tumbler, 5 oz., juice	18.00
Plate, 7⅜", salad	5.00	Tumbler, 9 oz., water	15.00
Plate, 9⅛", dinner	6.00	Tumbler, 12 oz., iced tea	15.00

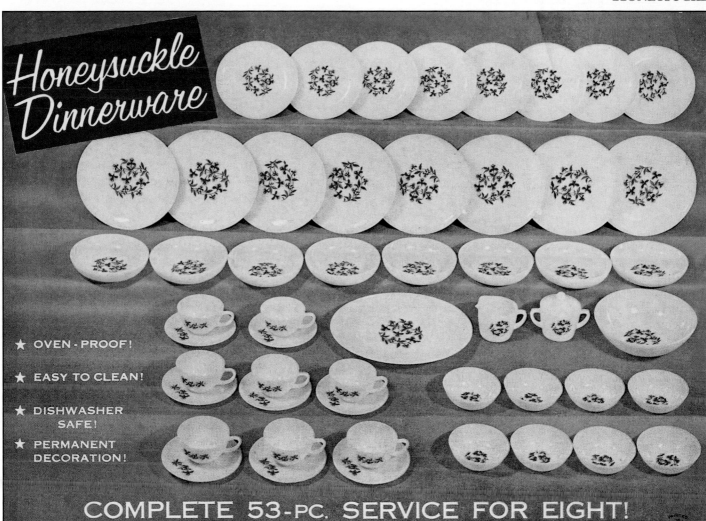

Honeysuckle Dinnerware

★ OVEN - PROOF!

★ EASY TO CLEAN!

★ DISHWASHER SAFE!

★ PERMANENT DECORATION!

COMPLETE 53-PC. SERVICE FOR EIGHT!

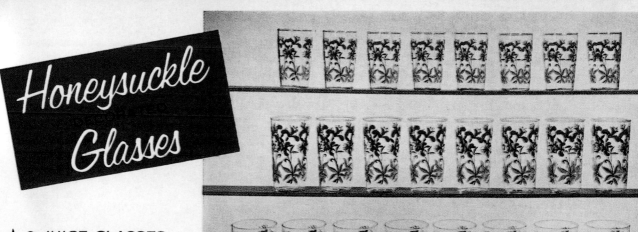

Honeysuckle Glasses

★ 8 JUICE GLASSES

★ 8 WATER GLASSES

★ 8 ICED TEAS

PR-7
4-59

COMPLETE 24-PC. SERVICE FOR EIGHT!

"JANE RAY" 1946 – 1965

Colors: amber, crystal, Ivory, Jade-ite, Peach Lustre, Vitrock

"Jane Ray" is a name that collectors have called this pattern and no one seems to know where the name originated. Even one of Anchor Hocking's employees asked me where I found the name "Jane Ray" to use in the book. It was established before I started writing books in 1972, and that was the same question I asked the dealer from whom I bought a full chicken box of Jade-ite at the Nashville flea market — for $15.00. Ah, the "good ol' days"!

For many beginners, "Jane Ray" is synonymous with Jade-ite; and until they start seriously collecting, they do not comprehend that there are different patterns of Jade-ite. If you look at the starter set boxes below, you will note that Anchor Hocking only called this pattern Jade-ite. That box with the orange background was one of the first styles of boxes used. The first Anchor Hocking catalog listing is in 1946 for a "Heat Resistant" cup and saucer. No mention of other pieces was made until the following year. Some pieces have rayed backs. Note the saucer shown on page 50 in the third row.

There are other colors of "Jane Ray." The dinner plate, cup, saucer, and dessert bowl can be found in Ivory that looks beige in the photo on page 49, particularly when compared to the Vitrock in the same picture. Vitrock "Jane Ray" is difficult to find; but there are fewer collectors searching for it than the ever-present Jade-ite. Add $5.00 to $25.00 for a boxed set depending on size and condition; and the Town Crier flour sack with "Jane Ray" pictured sells for $40.00.

The tidbit pictured at the bottom of page 49 is original and includes instructions of how to assemble it piece by piece. The box and instructions are as valuable as the glass.

The 9" flat rimmed soup is often confused with the 7⅝" regular soup plate, but I am not sure why. There is 1⅜" difference! The soups are shown in the bottom row on page 50 and pictured again in the Clarification section on page 218. The 6¼" plate is being confused with 5¾" saucers. There is no cup ring in the plate. They are shown side by side on page 51.

Demitasse sets are difficult pieces to find, and **demitasse saucers are harder to find** than the cups! Notice the amber demitasse set on page 169. Too, very few crystal demitasse sets have been found. In the middle of page 51 are a translucent Jade-ite cup and a rolled edge vegetable bowl. The rolled edge bowl is a factory worker's project and the cup was one of those bad batches of Jade-ite that collectors wish Hocking had not tossed aside as an inferior product.

	Jade-ite	Ivory	Vitrock
Bowl, 4⅞", dessert	12.00	25.00	10.00
Bowl, 5⅞", oatmeal	20.00		18.00
Bowl, 7⅝", soup plate	24.00		
Bowl, 8¼", vegetable	25.00		25.00
Bowl, 9", flat rimmed soup	250.00		
Cup	6.00	20.00	8.00
*Cup, demitasse	40.00		20.00
Creamer	10.00		
Plate, 6¼"	100.00		
***Plate, 7¾", salad	12.00		

	Jade-ite	Ivory	Vitrock
Plate, 9⅛", dinner	13.00	45.00	20.00
Platter, 9" x 12"	25.00		
Saucer	2.00	10.00	2.00
**Saucer, demitasse	45.00		20.00
Sugar	10.00		
Sugar cover	22.50		

* amber, crystal, Lustre – $12.50
** amber, crystal, Lustre – $22.50
***Hand-painted animals – $25.00

Dinnerware & Patterns

LACE EDGE 1959 – 1976

Colors: Milk White, Azur-ite

Lace Edge in Milk White was a long-term production by Anchor Hocking. Many of these items were sold for flower arrangements and were well distributed. Even my mother-in-law has one of these she puts flowers in for her kitchen table — and she is not a collector. The Lace Edge photo was very washed out in the last book; so we tried a colored background as well as buying some items with color. Some of the items photographed on blue were laid flat and the decorated designs cannot be seen. The divided relish in the fourth row and the bowl in the bottom row were decorated.

Hocking's original Lace Edge pattern is illustrated by the three Gay Fad Studios' plates with fruit in the foreground of the photo below. These decorations are more desirable to collectors than the later made Lace Edge. That Distlefink decorated item with the red bird is the most desirable decoration of Gay Fad on Lace Edge.

Many other Lace Edge pieces were used for decals and Grandma's artistic endeavors. That "Gene" painted plate was found by my wife, who was a grinning like a Cheshire cat when she presented it to me.

	*Milk White
** Bowl, 11", ftd.	15.00
Bowl, 9½"	15.00
Compote, 7" x 3½"	6.00
Compote, 7" x 6¼", w/cover	12.50
*** Plate, 8¼", salad	7.00

	*Milk White
**** Plate, 13", cake	15.00
***** Plate, 13", three-part relish	15.00
Relish, heart shaped (Azur-ite)	45.00
Sherbet, 5¼ oz.	3.50

* add 25% to 50% for decorated
** Primrose decal – $150.00
*** State plates – $15.00; Distlefink $35.00

**** Fleurette – $100.00
***** Fruit hand-painted Gay Fad – $75.00

LAUREL 1951 – 1965

Colors: Gray, Ivory, Ivory White, Jade-ite, Peach Lustre

For space saving purpose in this book, I have combined all colors of Laurel into one category even though Hocking only used Laurel for designating the gray.

Peach Lustre color/pattern was characterized as "The New Sensation" in a 1952 Anchor Hocking catalog. From its introduction as Peach Lustre until its demise in 1963, the name was used for the color as well as this pattern. One more laurel leaf design was christened Gray Laurel in a 1953 catalog. That is the only reference to Gray Laurel in Anchor Hocking records.

The Peach Lustre 11" serving plate was discontinued as of August 25, 1960. It is the most difficult piece to find, particularly with good color. The major aggravation to both of these colors is that the sprayed-on colors disintegrate. Each of these will show white streaks if used, scratched, or washed in strong detergents.

Page 56 shows three colors not accounted for in catalogs: Ivory, Ivory White, and Jade-ite. The Ivory Laurel is almost beige when pictured beside the Ivory White. The White creamer and sugar are pictured at the ends of the middle row on page 56. Only the five pieces priced below have been confirmed in White Laurel and the prices of each of these have risen considerably in the last two years.

Add $10.00 – 30.00 for a Gray Laurel box depending upon its condition. Please don't write about the pieces photographed with the six-piece place setting box at left. My photographer couldn't coax that "shy" soup plate out of the box! Add $3.00 for a Gray Laurel label and $1.00 for a Peach Lustre one.

The maroon and gray striped tumblers pictured at right are often found with Gray Laurel and were likely sold that way although I have not heard of any being found in boxes of Gray Laurel. Crystal stemware, like those shown under "Bubble," were also engraved with a Laurel cutting to go with these patterns.

	Ivory White	White	Gray Laurel	Peach Lustre
Bowl, 4⅞", dessert	12.00		7.00	4.00
Bowl, 7⅝", soup plate	25.00		16.00	10.00
Bowl, 8¼", vegetable	40.00		30.00	10.00
Creamer, ftd.	10.00	15.00	5.00	4.00
* Cup, 8 oz.	7.50	10.00	4.00	3.50
Plate, 7⅜", salad	15.00	18.00	8.00	9.00
Plate, 9⅛", dinner	20.00		10.00	5.00
Plate, 11", serving	40.00		20.00	**14.00
Saucer, 5¾"	3.50	5.00	3.00	1.00
Sugar, ftd.	10.00	10.00	5.00	4.00

* Jade-ite – $195.00
** No wear

Dinnerware & Patterns

Anchorglass *makes your dream-table come true!*

Imagine! A Dinnerware Service for 4...RICH, GRAY LAUREL...

GOLDEN PEACH LUSTRE...GLOWING JADE-ITE

about $279 *complete*

18-PIECE GIFT-PACKED SERVICE-FOR-4 SET... ABOUT $2.79
4 CUPS, 4 SAUCERS, 4 DESSERTS, 4 DINNER PLATES, CREAMER, SUGAR

18-PIECE GIFT-PACKED SERVICE-FOR-4 SET... ABOUT $2.79
4 CUPS, 4 SAUCERS, 4 DESSERTS, 4 DINNER PLATES, CREAMER, SUGAR

20-PIECE GIFT-PACKED SERVICE-FOR-4 SET... ABOUT $2.79
4 CUPS, 4 SAUCERS, 4 DESSERTS, 4 SALAD PLATES, 4 DINNER PLATES

...and they are heat-proof
...will not "craze"!

Now! You can set your table—company style—with your choice of the glamorous new dinnerware patterns pictured here! And, wonder of wonders, these gleaming pieces are as strong and practical as they are low in price.

Don't put off the luxury of setting a lovely table one second longer. See this lovely Anchorglass dinnerware, wherever glassware is sold. If your dealer does not have this tableware in stock, he can get it for you by writing Anchor Hocking Glass Corporation.

All dinnerware pieces are available individually in open stock at low prices...for instance, cups and saucers, only 10¢ each!

Look for the name **Anchorglass**   Guaranteed by Good Housekeeping

A PRODUCT OF ANCHOR HOCKING GLASS CORPORATION • LANCASTER, OHIO

Dinnerware & Patterns

MEADOW GREEN 1967 – 1977

Colors: White w/decal

Meadow Green was first illustrated in Anchor Hocking's 1967 catalog. There were both dinnerware and ovenware lines available. In the early years of production, a stacking cup, creamer, and sugar were manufactured which have a black or darker green bottom that is hidden if stacked. In 1970, the darker bottomed items gave way to the newer style pictured in the top row. I observe more of the darker bottomed stacking sets in my travels, but they were only made for four years and should be more scarce! Mixing bowls were made as late as 1977, but I have seen very few of them.

Meadow Green's design does have a proclivity to fade in color with use, but does not seem to erode as readily as do some of the 1960s wares. The labels found on Meadow Green dishes say Dimension Dinnerware. Yet, I find no reference in Anchor Hocking's catalogs to the pattern other than with the Meadow Green name. I have never seen a Meadow Green label. Add $3.00 to the price for those labels.

	White w/decal		White w/decal
Bowl, 4⅝", dessert	3.50	Casserole, 3 qt., w/crystal cover	10.00
Bowl, 5", cereal, 8 oz.	3.00	Creamer, two styles	3.00
Bowl, 6⅝", soup	6.00	Cup	2.50
Bowl, 8¼", vegetable	12.00	Custard, 6 oz.	1.50
Bowl, 1½ qt., mixing	6.00	Loaf pan, 5" x 9"	6.50
Bowl, 2 qt., mixing	8.00	Mug, 8 oz.	3.00
Bowl, 2½ qt., mixing	10.00	Plate, 7⅜", salad	2.50
Cake dish, 8", square	6.00	Plate, 10", dinner	4.00
Cake dish, 9" round	6.50	Platter, 12" x 9"	8.00
Casserole, 12 oz., hdld.	3.50	Saucer	.50
Casserole, 1 qt. w/crystal cover	7.00	Sugar w/lid, two colors	7.00
Casserole, 1½ qt. w/crystal cover	8.00	Utility dish, 1½ qt.	6.00
Casserole, 1½ qt., oval w/crystal cover	8.00	Utility dish, 2 qt.	7.00
Casserole, 2 qt., w/crystal cover	9.00		

Dinnerware & Patterns

PARK AVENUE 1987 – 1993

Colors: Crystal, blue

Park Avenue was a new pattern line introduced by Anchor Hocking in 1987 to "re-create the Glamour Era of 1938 when Anchor Hocking first introduced a classic" (Manhattan) according to the 1987 Inspiration catalog issued by the company. **None of the Park Avenue pieces are exactly like the old Manhattan.** Some, unfortunately are very similar, including the cereal bowl, dinner plate, salad plate, and comport. Manhattan was not originally made in blue or green (except the green footed tumbler) as Park Avenue has been. I am showing all the new pieces recently made in green.

Many collectors of older Manhattan have bought Park Avenue to use as everyday dishes. Manhattan's collectibility had not been influenced by the making of Park Avenue until recently. The cereal bowls caused confusion, but the dinner plate and salad plates have caused irritation and aggravation to many longtime collectors. The **new plates measure exactly 8" and 10"**; so, if any plates you have bought in the last year are **even** inches, then you probably have bought some Park Avenue. Go to your local retail store and check them out. Dinner plates retail for less than $3.00 and salads for less than $2.00.

The 1938 Manhattan cereals are 5¼" wide and rarely seen, particularly in mint condition. Park Avenue's bowl is 6" wide. All original Manhattan bowls measure 1¹⁵⁄₁₆" high. If the bowl you have measures more than 2" high, then you have a piece of Park Avenue! The blue bowl above is Park Avenue; the crystal Manhattan cereal is beside it.

The new and old comports are pictured at right. The crystal one is new and the pink is old. Count the wafers or spools on the stem. **The new has five wafers and the old only has four.** That is the only major discernible difference.

Page 62 shows a catalog page with the original Park Avenue pieces listed.

Park Avenue

The Glamour Era Re-Created anew in Park Avenue. We are utilizing special mold equipment to give you the high quality this line deserves.
It is a consumer "step up" choice. Be sure to see pages 4 and 5 for more items! We've also added the dimension of Sapphire color in the total offering!

Dinnerware & Patterns

Park Avenue

SAPPHIRE BLUE PARK AVENUE BEVERAGEWARE SINGLE PACKS

A. BB510BS 10 oz. Rocks, 1 dz.,
9#, (.40). $ _____ each.

B. BB511BS 9.5 oz. All Purpose Goblet, 1 dz.,
11#, (.62). $ _____ each.

C. BB512BS 12 oz. Beverage, 1 dz.,
12#, (.49). $ _____ each.

D. BB516BS 16 oz. Iced Tea, 1 dz.,
14#, (.61). $ _____ each.

FOUR-PACK SETS

E. BB510CB 4 pc. 10 oz. Rocks, 4 st.,
12#, (.57). $ _____ set.

F. BB511CB 4 pc. 9.5 oz. All Purpose Goblet, 4 st.,
15#, (.86). $ _____ set.

G. BB512CB 4 pc. 12 oz. Beverage, 4 st.,
16#, (.68). $ _____ set.

H. BB516CB 4 pc. 16 oz. Iced Tea, 4 st.,
18#, (.84). $ _____ set.

Simply exceptional clarity and brilliance show in every respect of this line whose classic looks will last through decades to come. Sapphire glass color befits the deco styling. Fluid circles and ridges trap the hues of iridescent sapphire blue. The rich result is pure geometry—totally unique for today's marketplace.

SAPPHIRE BLUE PARK AVENUE SERVINGWARE BULK

I. BB513 13 oz. Footed Dessert, 1 dz.,
14#, (1.42). $ _____ each.

J. BB525 6 in. Small Bowl, 1 dz.,
13#, (.84). $ _____ each.

K. BB530 10 in. Serving Bowl, ½ dz.,
23#, (2.05). $ _____ each.

L. BB539 8 in. Snack Plate, 1 dz.,
12#, (.63). $ _____ each.

M. BB550 13 in. Platter, ½ dz.,
20#, (.87). $ _____ each.

ENCLOSED GIFT CARTONS

N. BB500/334 4 pc. 6 in. Small Bowl, 6 st.,
29#, (1.81). $ _____ set.

O. BB500/337 1 pc. 10 in. Bowl, 4 st.,
17#, (1.44). $ _____ set.

P. BB500/343 1 pc. 13 in. Platter, 6 st.,
22#, (.88). $ _____ set.

Q. BB500/346 4 pc. 8 in. Snack Plate, 6 st.,
25#, (1.20). $ _____ set.

R. BB500/335 4 pc. 13 oz. Footed Dessert, 4 st.,
19#, (1.80). $ _____ set.

SAPPHIRE ACCESSORIES BULK

S. BB529 6 in. Ash Tray, 1 dz.,
15#, (.52). $ _____ each.

T. BB540 Salt/Pepper Shaker with chrome plated cap.
2 dz., 10#, (.24). $ _____ each.

U. BB541 9¾ in. Vase, ½ dz.,
19#, (1.38). $ _____ each.

ENCLOSED GIFT CARTONS

V. BB500/341 1 pc. 9¾ in. Vase, 6 st.,
21#, (1.41). $ _____ set.

W. BB500/340 2 pc. Salt & Pepper, 12 st.,
11#, (.31). $ _____ set.

X. BB500/347 2 pc. Footed Cake contains one 13 in. Footed Cake Plate and one 11¼ in. Dome. 2 st., 23#, (1.92). $ _____ set.

"PEACH BLOSSOM" MID 1950s

"Peach Blossom," as depicted here, was first thought to be from Gay Fad Studios as is the ovenware shown later in this book. As we studied this rendition of "Peach Blossom" and compared it to that of the Gay Fad ovenware decorations, however, we noted the following differences. The paint on the dinnerware is not as resilient nor as bold. It wears off easily. The styling on the leaves and flowers has varied brush strokes. Once you have studied Gay Fad productions, you can spot them a mile away as they are consistent to a point of mechanical precision. Don't get me wrong, I would buy this dinnerware to go with a collection of Gay Fad in a heartbeat. The only problem is finding a set to buy. The dinnerware shown here came from a collector in Minnesota and from a dealer in Lancaster, Ohio.

There are two and possibly three patterns of Fire-King used to make up this "Peach Blossom." "Bubble" was used as a serving bowl and that is a recognizable pattern. I suspect that 22K-gold (Anchorwhite Swirl trimmed with 22K) was used; but since gold was also added to the "Bubble" rim, it is possible that Anchorwhite Swirl was used and the gold trim was supplemented. I would have used that blank which already had the gold edging, but I do not know if re-firing the 22K after adding the "Peach Blossom" would have created a problem or not. If any of you crafters use kilns and know if you destroy the gold edge by re-heating, let me know.

I am sure that additional pieces will be found, but I will only price those pieces known at this time. All prices are for Swirl unless noted.

	Bowl, 4⅞", fruit or dessert	20.00
	Bowl, 8¼", vegetable	45.00
*	Bowl, 8⅜" vegetable	40.00
	Cup	35.00
	Plate, 7⅜", salad	15.00
	Plate, 9⅛", dinner	25.00
	Platter, 12" x 9"	50.00
	Saucer	10.00

* "Bubble"

PRIMROSE 1960 – 1962

Colors: White w/decal

Dinnerware & Patterns

Anchor Hocking employed the Primrose pattern to link dinnerware and ovenware for the first time. Primrose was made with pieces intended for either role. Although many of Anchor Hocking's lines were issued for dinnerware, they were often marked ovenware on the bottom to let customers know that they were "heat-proof" and could be "pre-warmed" in the oven. Primrose decals have had a tendency to wear over the years; look for pieces that have vivid color on the decals.

Primrose was only shown in the 1960 – 1961 and 1961 – 1962 catalogs For such a short lived pattern, Primrose has some experimental or limited production pieces which are driving collectors crazy trying to find. I pictured a shaker in the first book which collectors are not having much success locating; but would you believe a second style has surfaced? See page 67 for a comparison of these. The gravy boat, comports (on Lace Edge or Vintage blanks), and a vase are all pictured; however, I have not cornered the egg plate for photography as yet. White five and eleven ounce tumblers are being found; but the 9½ ounce and crystal tumblers are in seclusion.

All casserole covers for Primrose are crystal Fire-King and not white. The deep loaf pan was sold as a baking pan by adding a crystal glass cover. All the crystal glass lids are harder to find than their respective bottoms. Lids have a tendency to be dropped. Ovenware pieces were guaranteed against **oven breakage** for two years. Dealers would exchange a new item for the broken pieces.

The one quart casserole, baking pan, and oval casserole were all sold with a brass finished candle warmer and candle. Numerous readers have written to say that those brass holders are still working as they were intended! Consider $10.00 to $25.00 for a box and $3.00 – 5.00 for a label on Primrose. Boxed sets with tumblers are especially desirable. I can find no one who has seen a crystal, five ounce juice tumbler which should exist; if you should own one, please let me know.

	White w/decal		White w/decal
Bowl, 4⅝", dessert	3.50	Mug	75.00
Bowl, 6⅝", soup plate	9.00	Pan, 5" x 9", baking, w/cover	18.00
Bowl, 8¼", vegetable	14.00	Pan, 5" x 9", deep loaf	14.00
Cake pan, 8", round	12.00	Pan, 6½" x 10½", utility baking	12.00
Cake pan, 8", square	12.00	Pan, 8" x 12½", utility baking	35.00
Casserole, pt., knob cover	9.00	Plate, 7⅜", salad	5.00
Casserole, 1 qt., knob cover	12.00	Plate, 9⅛", dinner	7.00
Casserole, 1½ qt., knob cover	12.00	Platter, 9" x 12"	15.00
Casserole, 1½ qt., oval, au gratin cover	15.00	Saucer, 5¾"	1.00
Casserole, 2 qt., knob cover	16.00	Shaker, pr. (2 styles)	300.00
Comport, 10", ftd., Vintage	150.00	Sugar	5.00
Comport, 11", ftd., Lace Edge	150.00	Sugar cover	5.00
Creamer	5.00	Tray, 11" x 6", rectangular, snack	5.00
Cup, 5 oz., snack	3.00	Tumbler, 5 oz., juice (white)	30.00
Cup, 8 oz.	3.00	Tumbler, 4⅛", 9½ oz., water (white)	75.00
Custard, 6 oz., low or dessert	3.50	Tumbler, 10 oz., water (crystal)	50.00
Egg plate	150.00	Tumbler, 11 oz. (white)	25.00
Gravy or sauce boat	250.00	Vase	150.00

"RAINBOW" 1938 – EARLY 1950s

"Rainbow" tableware was first shown in Anchor Hocking's 1939 catalog, but Tangerine (red) ball jugs were introduced in the 1938 catalog. Along with Tangerine (2157) was Blue (2158), Green (2159), and Yellow (2160). For identification purposes, these are called Primary "Rainbow" colors and pictured on bottom of page 70, 71, and 72. The lighter colored Pastel "Rainbow" colors were designated Pink (159), Green (160), Yellow (161), and Blue (162).

We tried to have fun with this colorful pattern, and have included pieces other than dinnerware on page 69 and 71 to show you how this pattern can be expanded to use vases, flower pots, bulb bowls, and even a lamp. The "Rainbow" dinnerware below and on page 70 is shown mixed for that rainbow effect that collectors have been touting. This pattern adapts very well to that purpose, making Anchor Hocking either 60 years ahead of a collecting trend or it is just coming around again!

Hexagonal shakers are pictured in the catalog, but I have not spotted any yet. I have separated the pricing into Pastel and Primary headings; but to bring the prices listed, these pieces have to be mint. The stem listed (shown bottom of pg. 69) has a colored foot, but a crystal stem and bowl. These goblets were shown under Standard Glass Company listing in Anchor Hocking's 1940 catalog. They have cutting #112, called Criss-Cross & Punty, consisting of circular cuts and tic-tac-toe grids.

	*Pastel	Primary
Bowl, 5¼", utilty, deep		15.00
Bowl, 6", fruit	25.00	22.00
Bowl, 9½", vegetable		40.00
Creamer, ftd.	15.00	12.00
Cup	7.00	7.00
** Jug, 42 oz., ball	70.00	60.00
Jug, 42 oz., Manhattan	65.00	55.00
Jug, 54 oz.		60.00
Jug, 64 oz.		65.00
*** Jug, 80 oz., ball	60.00	50.00
Jug, 80 oz., ball, Pillar Optic		50.00
Plate, 6¼", sherbet	8.00	6.00
Plate, 7¼", salad	10.00	8.00
Plate, 9¼", dinner	15.00	12.00
Platter, 11"		40.00
Saucer	3.00	3.00
Shakers, pr.		25.00
Sherbet, ftd.	15.00	12.00
Stem, 10 oz., 7⅜"	10.00	

	*Pastel	Primary
Sugar, ftd.	15.00	12.00
Tumbler, 5 oz., fruit juice		12.00
Tumbler, 9 oz., bath, straight		12.00
Tumbler, 9 oz., table	15.00	10.00
Tumbler, 15 oz., ftd.		15.00
Tumbler, 12 oz., 4¾" straight		35.00

ACCESSORY ITEMS

	*Pastel	Primary
Bulb bowl, 5½"	15.00	18.00
Cactus pot, 2¼", round		8.00
Cactus pot, 2¼", square	20.00	20.00
Flower pot, 3¼"	18.00	15.00
Flower pot, 4", 2 styles	18.00	15.00
Lamp, 7" hurricane	35.00	
Vase, 3¾", 2 styles		10.00
Vase, 5¼", deco	15.00	12.00
Vase, 9", ruffled top	25.00	25.00
Water bottle, 54 oz.		30.00

* add 25% for green   **Tangerine $30.00   ***Tangerine $20.00

Dinnerware & Patterns

Dinnerware & Patterns

RESTAURANT WARE 1948 – 1967

Colors: Anchorwhite, Azur-ite, crystal, Jade-ite, Rose-ite

For a while, collectors and Internet auctions pushed the price of rare and hard-to-find restaurant items beyond the range of most collectors. After rocketing unbelievably high initially, many of these prices have now settled into a more reasonable level than they were. Jade-ite was being made twenty-four hours a day for years. Jade-ite Restaurant Ware was used in many churches, schools, fire stations, etc. The single biggest user, I'm told, was U.S. military bases. A former soldier told me he ate his vittles off Jade-ite while on base.

The stack of 5½" to 10" plates below shows all five sizes available. The pink cup is close to Rose-ite color and the Azur-ite fruit bowl is unusual for Restaurant Ware.

There are four platters in this pattern that are pictured side by side on page 219. The 8⅞" oval partitioned plate, **without an indent,** is the only rarely seen platter. The smaller 9½" and the larger 11½" platters can be found. I bought over 300 of the smaller ones from a Catholic church once. Most were sold for $3.00! One platter (9¾") has been dubbed the "football" platter because of its wider size. It is the first platter in second row on page 74. The 5" handled bowl and saucer are shown in the bottom row. That saucer's diameter is 7½".

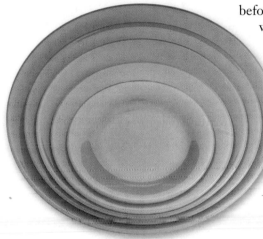

The five-compartment plate and the oval partitioned plates (already discontinued before 1953) are hard to find in mint condition. These were heavily used and severely worn pieces can be found! A ten ounce cereal fits on the partitioned plate.

The Jade-ite gravy in front of the platters is flat, but the commonly found white (page 75) is footed. The Jade-ite cup pictured to the right of the gravy has a G207 designation and is the cup most rarely seen. The first mug in the bottom row is frequently called a hot chocolate mug.

Crystal pieces of Restaurant Ware have recently begun to show up for sale at prices similar to white.

A note about the ball jug; they are not necessarily rare just desirable to many collectors. Over 300 of them have been listed on one Internet auction in the last couple of years. You do the math! Check any you find for cracks at the handle.

	Crystal/White	Jade-ite
*Bowl, 4¾", fruit, G294	8.00	12.00
Bowl, 5", handled		450.00
Bowl, 9¼", flat soup, G298	40.00	110.00
Bowl, 8 oz., flanged rim, cereal, G305	15.00	24.00
Bowl, 10 oz., deep, G309	20.00	28.00
Bowl, 15 oz., G300	18.00	28.00
Cup, demitasse		35.00
Cup, 6 oz., straight, G215	6.00	9.00
**Cup, 7 oz., extra heavy, G299	6.50	10.00
Cup, 7 oz., narrow rim, G319		12.00
Cup, 7 oz., tapered, G207		22.00
Gravy or sauce boat	30.00	500.00
Mug, coffee, 7 oz., G212, ex heavy	7.50	10.00
Mug, 6 oz., slim, chocolate		24.00
Pitcher, ball jug, G787		600.00
Plate, 5½", bread/butter, G315	6.00	12.00
Plate, 6¾", pie or salad, G297	6.00	12.00

	Crystal/White	Jade-ite
Plate, 8", luncheon, G316	20.00	60.00
Plate, 8⅞", oval partitioned (indent), G211		70.00
Plate, 8⅞", oval non-partitioned (indent), G310		85.00
Plate, 9", dinner, G306	15.00	24.00
Plate, 9⅝", 3-compartment, G292, tab or none	10.00	28.00
Plate, 9⅝", 5-compartment, G311		38.00
Plate, 10", serving		150.00
Platter, 9½", oval, G307	25.00	55.00
Platter, 9¾", oval, "football"		70.00
Platter, 11½", oval, G308	20.00	50.00
Saucer, 6", G295	3.00	4.00
Saucer, 7½", for hdld. bowl		150.00
Saucer, demitasse		40.00

*Azur-ite – $35.00   **Rose-ite – $150.00

ROYAL LUSTRE AND WHITE 1976 – 1977

Colors: Lustre and Anchorwhite

In 1976, the new Royal pattern was introduced reinstating the "Peach Lustre" color that was used from 1951 to 1965 on Laurel. Evidently, Lustre was not as accepted during the Bicentennial; so Anchorwhite was also produced. Both colors were discontinued by 1977, making the supply of both colors of Royal inadequate today.

I have found the Royal Lustre demitasse cups on "Jane Ray" saucers several times in antique malls, causing me to believe that some dealers do not realize that these are two different patterns. Although similar, the edges of Royal are scalloped and those of "Jane Ray" are not. Many of the Anchorwhite Royal pieces are more difficult to find than Lustre. The platter can be found; but, so far, a creamer and sugar cannot.

Note the Jade-ite plate below. It was listed as Jade-ite Royal on an Internet auction. It is Jade-ite, but, close examination shows it only similar to the Royal pattern.

	Lustre	Anchor-white
Bowl, 4¾", dessert	6.00	5.00
Bowl, 6⅜", soup plate	9.00	8.00
Bowl, 8½", vegetable	25.00	20.00
Bowl, 9", flat rimmed soup	20.00	20.00
Cup	8.00	7.00
Cup, demitasse	12.00	15.00
Creamer	7.50	
Plate, 7⅜", salad	7.00	7.00
Plate, 10", dinner	12.00	12.00
Platter, 9½" x 13"	30.00	40.00
Saucer	2.00	2.00
Saucer, demitasse	15.00	8.00
Sugar	10.00	
Sugar cover	8.00	

Dinnerware & Patterns

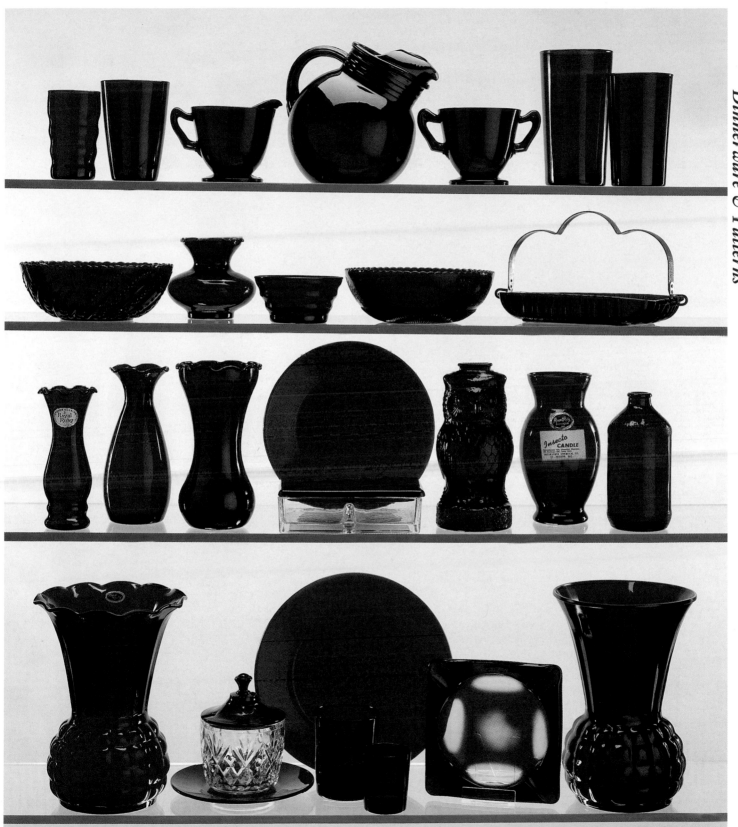

Dinnerware & Patterns

Colors: Desert Gold, 1961 – 1964; Forest Green, 1956 – 1960s; pink, 1939 – 1940; Royal Ruby, 1938 – 1939; White/Ivory (opaque), 1957 – 1960s

Dinnerware & Patterns

Amber Sandwich seems to be attracting new clientele to its ranks; and the one question I keep being asked is, "Where can I find a footed tumbler?" I wish I knew, but I have only owned one which was shown in some of my earlier books. A collector's friend talked me out of it a few years ago, for a well-received Christmas present that year. You will be able to assemble an amber set of Sandwich without great difficulty except for those tumblers. Only the cookie jar, 9" salad bowl, and 12" sandwich plate are hard to find and most admirers of this pattern only want one each of those.

Forest Green Sandwich dinner plates **continue** to rise in price. I figured that once they reached the $100.00 barrier, that that price would stick around for a while as it does for most patterns. While it did slow down for a spell, the Forest Green dinner plate has smashed through that barrier with ease and is now selling in the $130.00 range. All the harder to find pieces have slowed down their meteoritic escalation since new collectors have balked at starting a pattern with such high prices. Demand is the **major** reason that prices rise with scarcity adding to that.

Forest Green pitcher supplies are slim by virtue of a major marketing mistake. Juice and water tumblers were received free in oats. Nevertheless, **pitchers** were **only** available with sets of six tumblers! Anyone who ate oats already had more tumblers than they could use; so, they would not buy sets just to acquire the pitcher!

The rolled edge custard cup shown in the top row is extremely rare. At present, this is the only one to be found. A factory worker turned down the edge of a sherbet while it was still hot from the mould. Note that it is a little off kilter, so the worker probably was not used to that type of work.

There are more Forest Green cups available than saucers; so, prices for saucers have reached the price of cups. There are few patterns where saucers are harder to find than cups, but Forest Green Sandwich is one of them. No Forest Green Sandwich sugar or cookie jar lids have ever been found. Some former employees remembered topless cookie jars being sold as vases.

I thought only bowls were made in pink, but a very light pink juice pitcher has been found. It is pictured on page 86. While looking at that page, notice the plastic Sandwich pieces in the top row. If anyone has information on these plastic sets, please let me know.

The yellow salad plate and cup are thanks to Anchor Hocking. A crystal opalescent bowl is pictured on page 86.

Note the boxed set of Forest Green on page 86. In particular, notice the artist's rendition of the straight sided pieces that are actually rounded. That is only one reason that catalog drawings of old can cause headaches when researching glassware!

In Kentucky, in the mid 1960s you could buy the Ivory (with gold trim) punch bowl set for only $2.89 along with an oil change and lubrication at Marathon gas stations. Crystal pieces were available free with a $3.00 gasoline purchase. Cathy and I ate many a meal off the salad plates when we first married in 1964. We had to have gas to get to work and the plates were free. Those we could afford!

	Desert Gold	Royal Ruby	Forest Green	Pink	Ivory/White
Bowl, 4⁵⁄₁₆", smooth			6.00		
Bowl, 4⅞", smooth	3.00	16.00		4.00	
Bowl, 5¼", scalloped	6.00	20.00		7.00	
Bowl, 5¼", smooth				7.00	
Bowl, 6½", smooth	6.00				
Bowl, 6½", scalloped		27.50	60.00		
Bowl, 6¾", cereal	12.00				
Bowl, 7⅝", salad			75.00		
Bowl, 8¼", scalloped		40.00	100.00	27.50	
Bowl, 9", salad	30.00				
Cookie jar and cover	37.50		*30.00		
Creamer			30.00		
Cup, tea or coffee	3.50		20.00		
Custard cup			3.00		
Custard cup, rolled edge			95.00		
Custard cup liner			2.50		
Pitcher, 6", juice			225.00	350.00	
Pitcher, ½ gal., ice lip			495.00		
Plate, 9", dinner	10.00		130.00		
Plate, 12", sandwich	15.00				
Punch bowl, 9¾"					15.00
Punch bowl stand					15.00
Punch cup					2.00
Saucer	3.00		20.00		
Sugar, no cover			27.50		
Tumbler, 3³⁄₁₆", 5 oz., juice			4.00		
Tumbler, 9 oz., water			5.00		
Tumbler, 9 oz., footed	250.00				

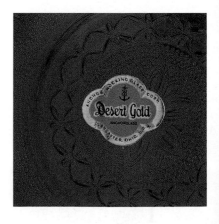

* no cover

SANDWICH CRYSTAL 1939 – 1966, 1977 – 1993

Anchor Hocking's Sandwich had a very long manufacturing period, so many pieces were copiously produced. I mentioned the premium give-aways under Sandwich colors on page 84. I'm sure that there were other areas of the country that had their own promotions. The smaller pieces of this pattern were excellent choices to fit inside boxes of merchandise.

I stated that the listed 9" salad bowl was the same bowl as the punch bowl; but a collector has written to emphasize that they are different. Has anyone else noticed differences in these two bowls? He says you can sit the 9" salad bowl in the punch bowl which measures 9¾"! He believes that the base for the punch bowl is rare because too many people are looking for a base to the 9" salad bowl and not a punch bowl. If your bowl measures exactly 9", then it is the salad bowl and not the punch bowl. The stand for the punch bowl is harder to find than the punch bowl itself. This might be one explanation; however, the punch set was also sold without a stand. If a boxed set of the punch bowl and cups is in your possession, measure the bowl and see if maybe the 9" bowl was packed in those sets. The 12" sandwich plate has become harder to find now that so many collectors are buying this pattern. This plate was also used as a liner for the 9" salad bowl. One collector says she uses these as serving plates for buffets and buys everyone she can find. Some of her friends have begun to admire her plates and now, she is buying them as gifts.

On the top row of page 88 there are two juice tumblers pictured. The smaller, three ounce juice is not being found in New England as it once was. The five ounce juice can be readily found. There is a price difference!

The 6½" cereal bowl with a scalloped top is shown third in row 2 on page 88. The regular cereal is pictured beside it for comparison. The regular custard and the crimped custard are shown side by side in that row. All the crimped and scalloped pieces had very limited production runs, and demand pushes their prices upward. The crimped pieces are listed as occasional Sandwich pieces only in the 1956 catalog.

Additional crystal pieces that are infrequently seen are the regular cereal, 5" crimped dessert bowl, and flawless dinner plates. That 5" crimped dessert listed by Anchor Hocking only measures 4⅞" in some cases. Mould variations make exact size listings a major problem!

Remember that Anchor Hocking reintroduced a crystal cookie jar in the late 1970s that was larger than the old. This jar was made for over 15 years and can be found occasionally in its original box. For a comparison of these cookie jars, I record measurements below. The newer one is currently selling in the $15.00 to $20.00 range.

	New	Old
Height	10¼"	9¼"
Opening width	5½"	4⅞"
Circumference/largest part	22"	19"

	Crystal
Bowl, 4⁵⁄₁₆", smooth	5.00
Bowl, 4⅞" – 5", crimped dessert	18.00
Bowl, 4⅞", smooth	6.00
Bowl, 5¼", scalloped	7.50
Bowl, 6½", smooth	7.50
Bowl, 6½", scalloped, deep	8.50
Bowl, 6¾", cereal	50.00
Bowl, 6¾", cereal, scalloped edge	150.00
Bowl, 7", salad	7.00
Bowl, 7⅝", scalloped	10.00
Bowl, 8¼", scalloped	12.00
Bowl, 8¼", oval	8.00
Bowl, 9", salad	23.00
Butter dish, low	45.00
Butter dish bottom	25.00
Butter dish top	20.00
Cookie jar and cover	40.00
Creamer	6.00
Cup, tea or coffee	2.50
Custard cup	3.50

	Crystal
Custard cup, crimped, 5 oz.	14.00
Custard cup liner	21.00
Pitcher, 6", juice	65.00
Pitcher, ½ gal., ice lip	85.00
Plate, 7", dessert	12.00
Plate, 8"	7.00
Plate, 9", dinner	20.00
Plate, 9", indent for punch cup	5.00
Plate, 12", sandwich	40.00
Punch bowl, 9¾"	20.00
Punch bowl stand	30.00
Punch cup	2.25
Saucer	1.50
Sherbet, footed	8.00
Sugar	8.50
Sugar cover	15.00
Tumbler, 3⅜", 3 oz., juice	18.00
Tumbler, 3⁹⁄₁₆", 5 oz., juice	6.50
Tumbler, 9 oz., water	8.00
Tumbler, 9 oz., footed	35.00

SHELL 1965 – 1976

Colors: Aurora (mother of pearl), Jade-ite, Milk White, Milk White trimmed in gold, Peach Lustre

I have combined all of the Shell patterns into one section to simplify explanations. I also relented by using Aurora for the "mother of pearl" finish on this pattern, even though the only time that name was used was for Soreno on a transparent color and not opaque. Aurora Shell is shown at the top of page 98; the bottom of that page shows additional pieces of Aurora finished items that can be blended into use with Aurora Shell. Enjoy the pictures on the following pages as there is little room for explanation.

The scalloped edge on all Shell pieces defines this from Swirl patterns whose edges are not scalloped. See the Clarifications section on page 219 where these edges, as well as cup shapes, are shown.

Golden Shell (Milk White with 22K edge) is shown on page 95. Many pieces of this were used for souvenir items, decorative paintings, and decals such as the New York World's Fair plate shown in the bottom row. There are a couple of others on this page. I've seen several of the Cupid or angel tidbits. Someone found these to their liking for a marketing strategy.

Jade-ite Shell (Jade-ite dinnerware in English Regency styling) makes up page 96. Add $20.00 to $25.00 for a Jade-ite Shell mint box. Lustre Shell (Peach Lustre) is shown on page 97. We had two different tidbits at the photo session; so, we decided to show they came originally in more than one style. The demitasse set that was used to sell candles is also on page 97.

Boxes add $5.00 to $10.00 for Golden Shell or Peach Lustre sets. Labels on Jade-ite and Golden Shell are fairly common; they will only add $1.00 to $2.00 to the price listed. A label identifying the real name of the mother of pearl finish would be worth at least $30.00.

Jade-ite Shell is the most desirable Shell pattern for collectors at present, but many others would like to find a set of Aurora Shell which seems **very** limited. The platter and sugar lid are both hard to find in Jade-ite. The Jade-ite "go-with" oval vegetable is the same mould as those found in Forest Green and Royal Ruby. The 9" platter has not been found in any color except Lustre Shell.

	Golden Shell	Jade-ite Shell	Lustre Shell	Aurora Shell	Milk White
Bowl, 4¾", dessert	3.50	12.00	4.00	20.00	4.00
Bowl, 6⅜", cereal	10.00	25.00	10.00	22.00	
Bowl, 7⅝", soup plate	12.00	30.00	15.00	25.00	10.00
Bowl, 8½", oval vegetable		400.00			
Bowl, 8½", round vegetable	9.00	28.00	18.00	50.00	12.00
Creamer, ftd.	3.50	25.00	10.00	35.00	
Cup, 3¼ oz., demitasse	7.50		10.00	25.00	10.00
Cup, 5 oz., snack	3.25				
Cup, 8 oz.	3.25	10.00	5.00	15.00	
Plate, 7¼", salad	4.00	18.00	3.50	25.00	4.00
Plate, 10", dinner	6.00	25.00	7.00		7.00
Plate, 10", snack w/indent	6.00				
Platter, 9", oval			40.00		
Platter, 9½" x 13", oval	9.00	85.00			
Platter, 11½" x 15½", oval			25.00		40.00
Saucer, 4¾", demitasse	10.00		10.00	20.00	12.00
Saucer, 5¾"	1.00	4.00	2.00	15.00	
Sugar, ftd.	4.00	25.00	10.00	25.00	
Sugar cover	4.00	75.00	8.00	35.00	

Dinnerware & Patterns

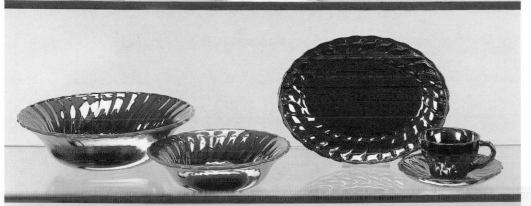

SORENO 1966 – 1970

Colors: Aquamarine, Aurora, Avocado, blue crystal, Honey Gold, Lustre (Amber, Blue, Cranberry, Smoke) Mardi-Gras, Milk White

Soreno was a contemporary glassware during the years that new kitchens were being decorated with avocado and harvest gold appliances. Anchor Hocking designers were well aware of color trends and Soreno was one of their answers. Avocado and Honey Gold are the Soreno colors most often encountered, but a few pieces were made in other colors, including Aquamarine, Mardi-Gras, Aurora, and Lustre. Aurora is the mother of pearl finish made in 1968 and illustrated by the pitcher in bottom row of page 100. Lustre appeared in 1967 on Amber, Blue, Cranberry, and Smoke.

Soreno is a pattern you either love or hate. Most of us who lived through avocado colored kitchens do not highly prize those colors of Soreno, today. Page 101 shows some boxed sets and one use of a vase as a humidor and pipe holder. (I paid $5.00 for the one shown, but have seen several priced for a lot more which were not selling!) Boxes fetch $3.00 to $10.00 with Aurora boxes the higher end and Avocado and Honey Gold the lower end.

The painted daisy center handled server is showing up occasionally. Pieces to watch for include any color other than Avocado, Honey Gold, crystal, and Milk White. Patio lamps and 14" plates seem to be in demand even in those colors. All patio oil lamps have crystal bases and crystal or colored chimneys. If you like the colors, this is a vast, inexpensive, and available pattern to pack away for the future.

	Aquamarine	Avocado Milk White	Crystal	Honey Gold	Lustre, MardiGras Aurora
Ashtray, 4¼"	5.00	2.50		2.50	12.00
Ashtray, 6¼"	7.50	3.50		3.50	
Ashtray, 8"	10.00	5.00		5.00	20.00
Bowl, 4¾", chip/dessert	5.00	2.00	2.50		8.00
Bowl, 5½", cereal		4.00	4.50		
Bowl, 5⅞", salad/soup		5.00	5.50		
Bowl, 8½", chip/salad	10.00	6.00		6.50	14.00
Bowl, 11⅜", 4 qt.	15.00	7.50		8.00	18.00
Butter, ¼ lb. w/cover		6.00			
Creamer		3.00			
Cup, 7 oz.		2.00	2.50		4.00
Patio lamp base, 5" tall			10.00		
Patio lamp chimney, 7" tall		5.00	4.00	6.00	25.00
Plate, 10", luncheon		3.00			
Plate, 10", snack w/indent		2.50	3.00		5.00
Plate, 11", serving		5.00			
Plate, 14", serving		6.00			
Pitcher, 28 oz., juice	12.00	6.00	7.00	6.00	
Pitcher, 64 oz., water	18.00	7.50	8.00	7.50	20.00
Saucer		.50	.75		
Shaker, pr.		4.00	6.00	5.00	
Sugar		3.00			
Sugar lid		1.00			
Tumbler, 6 oz., juice	5.00	2.00	2.50	2.50	5.00
Tumbler, 9 oz., on-the-rocks	6.00	2.50	3.00	3.00	6.00
Tumbler, 12 oz., water	7.00	3.00	3.50	3.50	7.00
Tumbler, 15 oz., iced tea	8.00	3.50	4.00	4.00	8.00
Vase, 6" x 7"		5.00			
Vase, 6⅞", bud		5.00			
Vase, 8", bulbous		7.50			
Vase, 9½"		7.00			
Water bottle, 48 oz., w/spout cap			6.00		

SWIRL (PART 1) 1949 – 1962

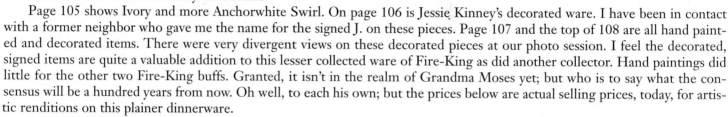

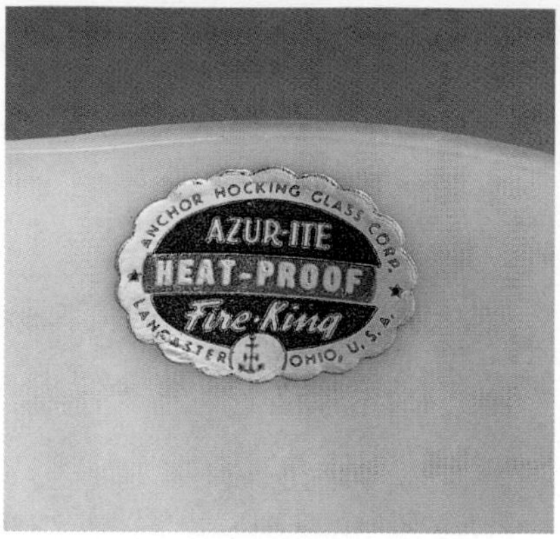

Colors: Azur-ite, Jade-ite, Anchorwhite, and Ivory, and with gold trims

Swirl patterns have been split into two sections. Part 1 illustrates Azur-ite Swirl, Ivory Swirl, White Swirl, Jade-ite Swirl, Golden Anniversary (22K trimmed Ivory Swirl), and 22K Gold (22K trimmed Anchorwhite Swirl). The **Swirl** name has been added by collectors to each pattern to distinguish them from other Anchor Hocking patterns. Anchor Hocking called both Charm and Swirl, Azur-ite. See label on right. Collectors need more specific names to identify various line numbers and patterns.

The top of page 103 shows the rare 9" flanged soup on the left and the regular soup on the right. Also, the gold decorated creamer is unusual. Boxed sets on page 103 show tumblers that were packed with Azur-ite Swirl. They came in three sizes: 5 ounce juice, 9½ ounce water, and 14 ounce tea, and presently sell from $15.00 to $20.00. Labels add $2.00 – 5.00 to the listed prices depending upon the item and color; and boxes can add $10.00 – $30.00.

Top of 104 shows Anchorwhite Swirl which is more difficult to find than most collectors realize. The flanged soup on the bottom left is one of the few Ivory ones found.

Page 105 shows Ivory and more Anchorwhite Swirl. On page 106 is Jessie Kinney's decorated ware. I have been in contact with a former neighbor who gave me the name for the signed J. on these pieces. Page 107 and the top of 108 are all hand painted and decorated items. There were very divergent views on these decorated pieces at our photo session. I feel the decorated, signed items are quite a valuable addition to this lesser collected ware of Fire-King as did another collector. Hand paintings did little for the other two Fire-King buffs. Granted, it isn't in the realm of Grandma Moses yet; but who is to say what the consensus will be a hundred years from now. Oh well, to each his own; but the prices below are actual selling prices, today, for artistic renditions on this plainer dinnerware.

Jade-ite Swirl is a rare pattern with only cups, saucers, dinner plates, and a platter being found. The platter is from Anchor Hocking's morgue. I kept hoping one would turn up to buy; but alas, one did not.

The top of page 109 shows Golden Anniversary and the bottom, 22K Gold. That platinum trimmed cup is Shell, not Swirl. It's the only piece of platinum-trimmed **Shell** I have seen; it seemed as good a place as any to show the different shapes of the cups of these two confusing patterns.

	Azur-ite	*Ivory/White	Jade-ite	Golden/22K Anniversary
Bowl, 4⅞", fruit or dessert	12.00	7.00		4.00
Bowl, 5⅞", cereal	22.00	24.00		
Bowl, 7⅝", soup plate	18.00	10.00		10.00
Bowl, oval vegetable				
Bowl, 8¼", vegetable	35.00	20.00		12.00
Bowl, 9¼", flanged soup	175.00	100.00		
Creamer, flat	**10.00	10.00		
Creamer, ftd.		2.75		3.25
Cup, 8 oz.	6.00	8.00	40.00	4.00
Custard cup, 8 oz.		25.00		
Plate, 7⅜", salad	9.00	8.00		6.00
Plate, 9⅛", dinner	10.00	10.00	80.00	7.50
Plate, 11", serving		25.00		
Platter, 12" x 9"	22.00	20.00	350.00	12.50
Saucer, 5¾"	2.00	2.00	20.00	1.00
Sugar, flat, tab handles	10.00	10.00		
Sugar, ftd., open handles		3.00		3.50
Sugar lid, for flat sugar	8.00	5.00		

* Quality hand-painted vegetable bowl – $50.00; cup/saucer – $35.00; dinner plate – $30.00
Decal decorated salad plate – $18.00; dinner plate – $20.00
** Gold decorated – $25.00

Dinnerware & Patterns

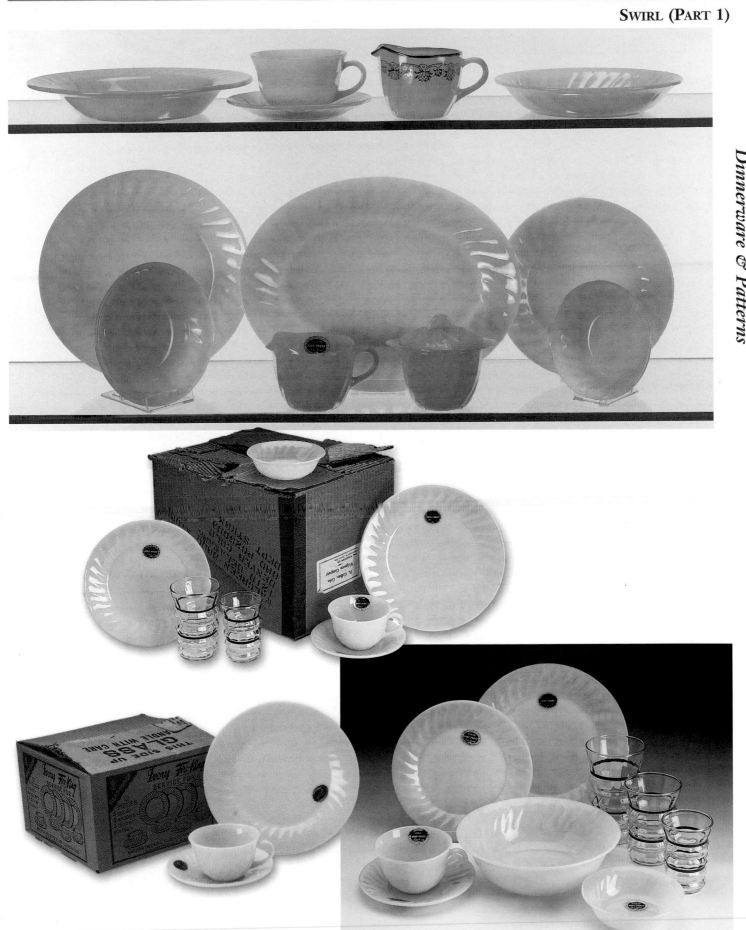

Dinnerware & Patterns

Dinnerware & Patterns

"THOUSAND LINE," "STARS & BARS," "RAINBOW STARS," 1941-1960s

Colors: Crystal, satinized colors, white

All items, save one, of this Anchor Hocking line are numbered between 1000 and 1090 in old catalogs. The candle holder is number 981, and is shown with "Stars & Bars" pattern. Actually, EAPC collectors have dipped into this line while searching for that pattern. The bud vase pictured is 1071 and not EAPC. All Early American Prescut pieces have catalog line numbers in the 700s. Many collectors buy the large salad bowl and tray to use for salads. Imagine that! These sets were originally sold with a glass fork and spoon. It was a popular gift item to new brides during W.W.II. and was promoted heavily during the war years. This older set can be found comparably priced to currently made glassware. Which would you rather buy?

I can only find the 8" salad plate listed in the 1942 catalog which may account for its scarcity today. Some other pieces were listed as late as the 1960s.

You will find some satinized pieces in "Thousand Line," and many of these will be color decorated. Add 50% to the price listed for ruby flashed. Satinized color adds to the appearance if well done, but sometimes pieces look rather haphazardly finished. Most "Thousand Line" pieces were abundantly distributed over twenty years; thus, it can be gathered with a little searching. This is a pattern that few yet recognize, just as were many of the Fire-King patterns only a few years ago. Now is the time to buy it. A plethora of sugar and creamers exist. An Anchor Hocking distributor must have really promoted them to restaurants.

Dinnerware & Patterns

	Crystal		Crystal
Bowl, 6", handled jelly	10.00	Plate, 8", salad	10.00
Bowl, 7½", shallow	10.00	Plate, 12", cake	13.00
Bowl, 8", deep, vegetable	12.00	Plate, 12½", sandwich	13.00
Bowl, 9¼", fruit, 3-ftd.	15.00	Relish, 7½" three-part, round	8.00
Bowl, 10½", salad, flat base, 7" ctr.	25.00	Relish, 12", six-part	13.00
Bowl, 10⅞", vegetable, rim base, 5½", ctr.	15.00	Relish, 10", two-handled, oval	6.00
Candle, 4"	3.00	Spoon	7.50
Candy w/lid	17.00	Sugar, 2½"	4.00
Creamer, 2½"	4.00	Tray, 12½", sandwich	12.00
Fork	7.50	* Vase, bud	12.00

* white $10.00

115

Colors: Burgundy, Ivory, Jade-ite, Peach Lustre

"Three Bands" is not an official Anchor Hocking name for this smaller pattern, but it's illustrative and memorable. Because of that traditional name, I have dubbed a couple of other Jade-ite patterns "One Band" and "Two Bands." If factory names for these patterns should be unearthed, I will incorporate them in the future.

Peach Lustre "Three Bands" cups and saucers are frequently found; so frequently, in fact, that no one thought to bring one to the photography session! I had to go buy a set for the photo at the last minute. All other pieces of "Three Bands" are prized by collectors. This is another pattern that cannot be collected as a large set; but, most Fire-King collectors want a sample of each piece or color.

I explained about the discovery of the Burgundy name in the first book. Prices have soared for pieces of Burgundy. It is another color, I was told, that Anchor Hocking had trouble producing and as such was never marketed. Notice the three cups pictured on page 117 that illustrate the problems with this color. The first cup is Swirl and the others are "Three Bands." The mix on the Swirl cup reminds me of Oxblood Akro Agate which collectors view so fondly in children's dishes. The second cup has a white band on the edge and the other is normal. It's a good thing that the printing of labels preceded production or we would never have known of the Burgundy or Rose-ite names. A Burgundy label will add at least $15.00 to the price listed.

Labels on other "Three Bands" pieces say Ivory and Jade-ite as those found on most Jade-ite wares of the early 1950s. These labels add $2.00 to $4.00 to the price listed. The Jade-ite "Three Bands" dinner plate has now been found. See it on page 117.

A few "One Band" cup and saucers are being discovered, but only one "Two Bands" chili bowl has ever been seen.

	Burgundy	Ivory	Jade-ite	Lustre
Bowl, 4⅞", fruit or dessert	100.00	10.00		
Bowl, 5", chili (two bands)			250.00	
Bowl, 8¼", vegetable	500.00	50.00	95.00	
Cup, 8 oz.	75.00	12.50	50.00	3.00
Cup (one band)			200.00	
Saucer, 5¾"		5.00	75.00	1.00
Saucer (one band)			75.00	
Plate, 9⅛", dinner	300.00	25.00	500.00	

Dinnerware & Patterns

TURQUOISE BLUE 1956 – 1958

Turquoise Blue was approved as dinnerware, but all pieces are marked ovenware except for the egg plate which is not marked. A preponderance of Anchor Hocking's dinnerware lines are marked ovenware. Consumers recognized these items could be heated in the oven before using. Turquoise Blue's ovenware pieces are pictured throughout the remainder of the book.

Basic dinnerware pieces such as cups, saucers, 9" dinner plates, creamers, and sugars are easily found. The 6⅛" plates are as limited as the 10". Several collectors have told me they have never seen either one! That 10" plate is a better dinner plate than the 9" one promoted as a dinner.

Shown on this page are three different labels being found on Turquoise Blue. The Turquoise Anchorglass at left is the first one of those I have seen. Labels add $2.00 to $5.00 depending upon the piece to which it is attached.

On the next page are several interesting items. The basketweave bowl is pictured beside a bowl of the same mould shape without the basketweave design. Those basketweave bowls have reached in excess of $125.00 in today's marketplace. The boxed ice bucket proves that they were really sold that way. Another style ice bucket with a hinged lid is also pictured. Either bucket is pushing the $75.00 range, but the box is worth at least $25.00 alone. A vegetable bowl is also being found in a hammered aluminum holder. The late 1950s saw quite a few products promoted in hammered aluminum holders. There is a collecting society searching for just those aluminum items. The boxed dinner set is unusual and the box itself is worth $20.00 to $25.00. Boxes for snack sets are plentiful and only add $5.00 to the set price.

The 9" plate with cup indent used for a snack plate is usually found 22K gold trimmed. Some collectors do not want to mix the gold-trimmed pieces with their sets and others do not like snack sets; there are more snack sets for sale than are wanted right now. Do not put any gold-edged pieces in the microwave because the gold causes sparks. All other pieces worked well in our microwave when we used this set for our daily dishes.

Bowl, 4½", berry	10.00		Mug, 8 oz.	10.00
Bowl, 5", cereal or chili, 2⅜" high	15.00		Plate, 6⅛"	18.00
Bowl, 5", cereal (thin), 2" high	45.00		Plate, 7¼"	12.00
Bowl, 5", "Davy Crockett" style	100.00		Plate, 9"	12.00
Bowl, 6⅝", soup/salad	25.00		Plate, 9", w/cup indent	6.00
Bowl, 8", vegetable	22.00		Plate, 10"	30.00
Creamer	8.00		Saucer	1.50
Cup	5.00		Sugar	8.00

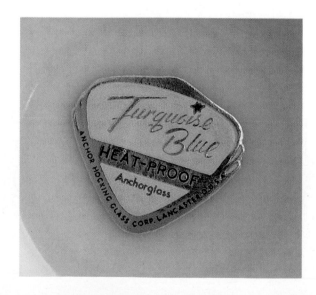

VIENNA LACE 1972 – 1976

Colors: White w/decals

Vienna Lace was listed only as a dinnerware gift set in Anchor Hocking's catalogs from 1972 to 1976. The only way Vienna Lace could be bought was by the set of 20 or 45 pieces. It was not an open stock pattern; thus, you could not order individual pieces to supplement a set.

Vienna Lace may be overlooked by collectors for a couple of reasons, but mainly, because the pattern does not show on some of the pieces. You could bypass the cup, saucer, creamer, or sugar if you are looking for the Vienna Lace pattern on them. I forgot to mention last book that some sets may have come with pieces that have a platinum edge only. The platter, plate, and straight-sided cereal were all found with sets of Vienna Lace. I can find no records in catalogs indicating this occurrence, but it seems to have happened. Another possibility is that since Vienna Lace was only sold in sets, these may have been the only replacement pieces available.

The sugar and creamer are the stacking style, but the cup is not. The cup is straight sided and non-tapered, almost like a mug. Also, the small bowl only has the center star of the decal. The bowl was too small to accommodate the entire Vienna Lace motif.

Prices are for pieces with pattern. Pieces with platinum edge only deduct 40% to 50%.

Bowl, 4⅝", dessert	5.00	Plate, 10", dinner	7.00
Bowl, 5", cereal (no design)	4.00	Platter, 9" x 12"	17.00
Bowl, 6⅝", cereal/soup	8.00	Saucer, 5¾"	2.00
Bowl, 8¼", vegetable	17.00	Sugar (no design)	5.00
Creamer (no design)	7.00	Sugar cover	5.00
Cup, 8 oz. (no design)	4.00		

Dinnerware & Patterns

WEXFORD 1967 – 2000

Colors: Crystal, assorted fired on decorations, Pewter Mist, green

Wexford caused some vociferous complaints from collectors who wished to see more pieces in the first book. I showed many catalog pictures with each piece identified, but some weren't happy with that. They wanted to see the real glass!

Wexford is classed as one of the "more" patterns in this book because it is not Fire-King. Introduced in 1967, Wexford has a few remaining pieces in production today. According to Anchor Hocking, the following pieces are still in production as of March 2000: 8½" ashtray, butter dish, cake stand and dome, creamer, punch set, salt/pepper (2 ounce and 8 ounce), and sugar/cover. A major chain store had an extensive sale on Wexford items during the recent holidays. Too, Cathy has now discovered a knock-off Wexford shaker labeled "Made in China."

The green pieces pictured here were in Wal-Mart for the Christmas season a few years ago. The cobalt cake stand and pink footed bowl do not seem plentiful. Many of the recently discontinued pieces are being sold by Big and Odd Lots stores. If you have one in your area, check it out. Collectors have suggested to me that the dinner plate, sherbet plate, oil lamp, captain's decanter (page 125, row 2, first item), candlesticks (sherbet style, bottom page 125), beer mug (last item, page 123), and lazy Susan are becoming difficult to find. The flashed Ruby (never called Royal Ruby) votive candle shown at right is one of five colors made besides crystal. The others are Green, Blue, Cranberry, and Amber. Pewter Mist is the gray color appearing on the top of page 123.

The Wexford oil lamp (hexagonal) that is shown in the catalogs is pictured on the top of page 125. A similar lamp (round) is pictured at the bottom of page 125, but I cannot find any records of this actually being Wexford. Anyone have an idea?

Wexford might be the next EAPC in the collecting world. It is only six years younger. We shall see what the year 2000 has in store for collecting trends.

	Crystal
Ashtray, 5½"	4.00
Ashtray, 8½"	6.00
Bowl, 5"	2.50
Bowl, 5½"	3.00
Bowl, 5¼", salad	3.50
Bowl, 6", salad	3.50
Bowl, 8", ftd. centerpiece	12.00
Bowl, 8¼", deep	9.00
Bowl, 9¾", salad/punch base	10.00
Bowl, 10", ftd. fruit	12.00
Bowl, 10", ftd. salad	10.00
Bowl, 14", serving	9.00
Bowl, 14", serving, scalloped top	10.00
Bowl, trifle (plain top)	10.00
Butter dish, ¼ lb.	3.00
Cake stand	15.00
Cake stand dome	6.00
Candle, 2½", votive	2.50
Candleholder, 5", pr.	35.00
Candy dish, 6¾" x 7¾", ftd./lid	12.00
Candy dish, 7¼", ftd./lid	12.00
Candy dish, floral bowl	6.00
Cigar/cigarette stand	35.00
Creamer, 8 oz.	2.50
Cruet, 5½ oz., w/stopper	3.00
Cup, 7 oz.,	2.00
Cup, 7 oz., punch or snack	2.00
Decanter, 32 oz.	12.00
Decanter, 32 oz., captain's	15.00
Goblet, 3 oz., cordial	2.00
Goblet, 3½ oz., cordial	2.50
Goblet, 5½ oz., wine/juice	2.50
Goblet, 9½ oz., water	3.00
Goblet, 10 oz., ftd	3.50
Ice bucket, w/cover	15.00

	Crystal
Jar, 17 oz., storage	3.00
Jar, 34 oz., storage	4.00
Jar, 58 oz., storage	5.00
Jar, 96 oz., with lid	12.50
Lazy Susan, 9 pc. (14" tray, 5¼" bowl, six 4"x5¾" inserts on swivel rack)	15.00
Mug, 15 oz.	6.00
Oil lamp	35.00
Pitcher, 18 oz., ftd.	10.00
Pitcher, 64 oz.	8.00
Plate, 6", dessert	3.00
Plate, 7¾", six-sided	7.00
Plate, 9½", dinner, scalloped edge	18.00
Plate, 9½", snack, indent	2.50
Platter, 12", round, serving	4.00
Platter, 14", round, serving	5.00
Punch bowl base, 9¾" (salad)	10.00
Punch bowl, 11 qt.	10.00
Relish tray, 5⅛" x 9⅞"	4.00
Relish, 11", 5 pt., center circle	6.00
Relish, 8½", 3 part	4.00
Saucer, 6"	1.00
Shakers, pr., 2 oz.	3.00
Shakers, pr., 8 oz.	3.00
Sherbet, 7 oz., stemmed	2.00
Sherbet, 7¼ oz., stemmed	1.50
Sugar cover	1.00
Sugar, 8 oz.	2.00
Tidbit, 9½" plate	5.00
Tidbit, two-tier, 6"/11" plates	10.00
Tray, 11", 5 pt., no center ring	9.00
Tray, 11", relish	4.00
Tumbler, 6 oz., wine/juice	2.00
Tumbler, 9½ oz., rocks	2.50
Tumbler, 10 oz. on-the-rocks	2.50

Dinnerware & Patterns

Tumbler, 11 oz., beverage	2.50	Vase, 6", bud or candlestick	3.00
Tumbler, 14 oz., double rocks	3.00	Vase, 9", bud	3.00
Tumbler, 15 oz., iced tea	3.50	Vase, 10½", ftd.	12.50
Tumbler, 16 oz., iced tea	3.50		

Dinnerware & Patterns

Dinnerware & Patterns

WEXFORD®

68666   68666
12" Platter
6 st. 18# .75

A

4567   28204
6" Wexford
Bud/Vase/
Candleholder
1 dz. 7# .54

B

4569   26734
Wexford 9" Bud
Vase
2 dz. 21# 1.34

C

4507F   36944
5.5 oz.
Cruet/Stopper
1 dz. 8# .43

D

4523   26732
Butter Dish/Cover
1 dz. 15# .62

E

4553E   27891
8 oz. Sugar/Cover
1 dz. 13# .73

F

4554E   27890
8 oz. Creamer
1 dz. 9# .58

G

54803   54803
2 pc. Candy
Dish/Cover
6 st. 20# 1.31

H

4552   03022
Candy Dish/Cover
1/2 dz. 20# 1.31

I

67312   67312
4 pc. Small Bowl
Set
6 st. 18# 1.33

J

67313   67313
9.75" Serving Bowl
4 st. 16# 1.57

K

67315   67315
Round Divided
Relish Set
6 st. 12# .60

L

68491   68491
Trifle Bowl Set
2 st. 13# .88

M

4525   26141
Salt / Pepper
2 dz. 9# .27
45893   45893
Salt/Pepper Set
12 st. 10# .35

N

4510EZ   57646
9.5 oz. Rocks
1 dz. 9# .38

O

4511EZ   57652
9.5 oz. Goblet
1 dz. 12# .55

P

4512EZ   57648
11 oz. Beverage
1 dz. 12# .47

Q

4526EZ   57650
15 oz. Iced Tea
1 dz. 14# .38
4526CWT   57651
4 pc. 15 oz. Iced
Tea Set
2 st. 11# .44

R

4564   09660
2 qt. Pitcher
1/2 dz. 27# 1.51

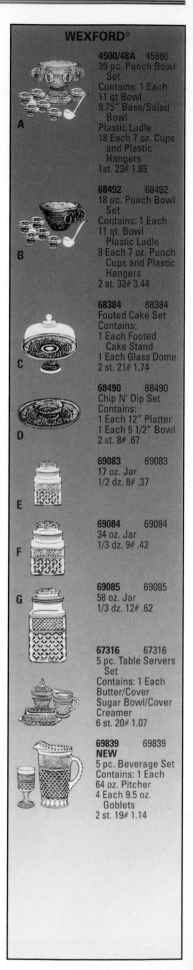

WEXFORD®

4500/48A   45886
39 pc. Punch Bowl
Set
Contains: 1 Each
11 qt Bowl
9.75" Base/Salad
Bowl
Plastic Ladle
18 Each 7 oz. Cups
and Plastic
Hangers
1 st. 23# 1.85

A

68492   68492
18 pc. Punch Bowl
Set
Contains: 1 Each
11 qt. Bowl
Plastic Ladle
8 Each 7 oz. Punch
Cups and Plastic
Hangers
2 st. 32# 3.44

B

68384   68384
Footed Cake Set
Contains:
1 Each Footed
Cake Stand
1 Each Glass Dome
2 st. 21# 1.74

C

68490   68490
Chip N' Dip Set
Contains:
1 Each 12" Platter
1 Each 5 1/2" Bowl
2 st. 8# .67

D

69083   69083
17 oz. Jar
1/2 dz. 8# .37

E

69084   69084
34 oz. Jar
1/3 dz. 9# .42

F

69085   69085
58 oz. Jar
1/3 dz. 12# .62

G

67316   67316
5 pc. Table Servers
Set
Contains: 1 Each
Butter/Cover
Sugar Bowl/Cover
Creamer
6 st. 20# 1.07

69839   69839
NEW
5 pc. Beverage Set
Contains: 1 Each
64 oz. Pitcher
4 Each 9.5 oz.
Goblets
2 st. 19# 1.14

IMPORTED LEAD CRYSTAL
GRACIOUSLY STYLED . . . FLAWLESSLY FASHIONED

WEXFORD®
SERVINGWARE

A

| 4525 | 26141 |
Salt/Pepper
2 dz. 9# (.27)

4500/81A 45893
2 pc. Salt & Pepper Set
12 st. 10# (.35)

B

| 4552 | 03022 |
Candy Dish/Cover
½ dz. 20# (1.31)

4500/242 54803
2 pc. Candy Dish/Cover
Set
6 st. 20# (1.31)

C

| 4553E | 27891 |
8 oz. Sugar/Cover
1 dz. 13# (.73)

D

| 4554E | 27890 |
8 oz. Creamer
1 dz. 9# (.58)

E
Bulk

| 4575H | 67319 |
5.25" Small Bowl
1 dz. 8# (.52)

4500/258 67312
4 pc. Small Bowl Set
6 st. 18# (1.33)

F

| 4571F | 67318 |
9.75" Serving Bowl
½ dz. 22# (1.19)

4500/259 67313
9.75" Serving Bowl Set
4 st. 16# (1.57)

G

| 4577 | 28214 |
14" Serving Bowl
½ dz. 29# (1.48)

4500/260 67314
14" Serving Bowl Set
4 st. 21# (2.05)

H

| 4598M | 67320 |
Round Divided Relish
1 dz. 20# (1.01)

4500/261 67315
Round Divided Relish Set
6 st. 12# (.60)

I

4500/262 67316
5 pc. Table Servers Set
Contains: 1 Each
Butter Dish/Cover
Sugar Bowl/Cover
Creamer
6 st. 20# (1.07)

J

4500/263 67317
5" x 9" Relish Set
6 st. 8# (.34)

K

| 4507F | 36944 |
5.5 oz. Cruet/Stopper
1 dz. 8# (.43)

L

| 4523 | 26732 |
Butter Dish/Cover
1 dz. 15# (.62)

4500/242
6-3/4 in. x 7-3/4 in.
Candy Dish/Cover
6 sets, 23 pounds
(1.62) cu. ft.
price

4500/243
10-1/2 in. Vase
6 sets, 32 pounds
(1.77) cu. ft.
price

4500/244
8 in. Footed
Centerpiece
6 sets, 29 pounds
(2.16) cu. ft.
price

4500/245
10 in. Footed
Fruit Bowl
6 sets, 36 pounds
(2.76) cu. ft.
price

4500/240
32 ounce Captain's
Decanter
6 sets, 19 pounds
(2.10) cu. ft.
price

4500/241
14 in. Serving
Platter
6 sets, 26 pounds
(1.23) cu. ft.
price

4500/67A
10 piece Wine
eight 5-1/2 ounce Stemmed
Wines, one 32 ounce
Decanter and stopper with
Sealing Feature
2 sets, 17 pounds
(.95) cu. ft.
price

4500/12A
7 piece Refreshment
six 11 ounce Beverages and
one 2 quart Pitcher
4 sets, 43 pounds
(2.13) cu. ft.
price

4500/148A
8 piece Bar
four 9-1/2 ounce Rocks, Ice
Bucket with Cover, Chrome-
plated Handle and Tongs
4 sets, 32 pounds
(2.07) cu. ft.
price

Wexford®

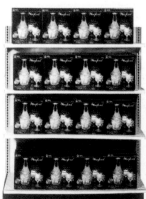

WHEAT 1962 – 1966

Wheat followed Primrose as a decaled dinnerware pattern that crossed into an ovenware line. Wheat reaped a harvest for Anchor Hocking beginning in 1962 and it is the most recognizable line made in the 1960s. Everyone growing up in the 1960s saw Mom or Grandma use a piece of Wheat just as the previous generation saw Sapphire Blue used. One catalog called it "Golden Wheat ovenware to go with our Wheat pattern." I see more dinnerware in my travels. Maybe the ovenware is still being used by Grandma!

The mug, chili bowl, and larger utility pan seem difficult to locate. The mug and chili bowl have seen some price hikes lately. It is to be hoped that you found yours before then. This is another pattern where time and use have taken their toll. I have seen a few pieces for sale that were nearly impossible to tell that the pattern was Wheat! If it's that bad, use it or give it away. If you cannot recognize the pattern, no collector will buy it — at these prices.

China companies were also making Wheat patterns during this era. Anchor Hocking combated this by advertising that their Wheat would not crack or craze. Tumblers are found in 5 ounce and 11 ounce sizes. A boxed set of ovenware and one of dinnerware are shown here. Boxed sets of dinnerware seem to be scarce. Not everyone needed several sets of ovenware and any extra gift sets were stored away for future use. Taking back gifts was not as common place then, as now. Boxes run from $10.00 to $20.00 for Wheat sets.

Both the oval and round 1½ quart casseroles and the 10½" baking pan were used with candle warmers. These candle warmers were brass finished with walnut handles. Warmers sell in the $6.00 to $8.00 range. Most of these were never used and can be found with the candles intact! New candles can be located at most kitchenware or hardware stores if you have a desire to try these out. Old candles did not survive well in Florida's climate.

	White w/decals			White w/decals
Bowl, 4⅝", dessert	3.50	Mug		50.00
Bowl, 5", chili	25.00	Pan, 5" x 9", baking, w/cover		16.00
Bowl, 6⅝", soup plate	8.00	Pan, 5" x 9", deep loaf		12.00
Bowl, 8¼", vegetable	12.00	Pan, 6½" x 10½" x 1½", utility baking		12.00
Cake pan, 8", round	11.00	Pan, 8" x 12½" x 2", utility baking		18.00
Cake pan, 8", square	10.00	Plate, 7⅜", salad		8.00
Casserole, 1 pt., knob cover	8.00	Plate, 10", dinner		6.00
Casserole, 1 qt., knob cover	10.00	Platter, 9" x 12"		14.00
Casserole, 1½ qt., knob cover	11.00	Saucer, 5¾"		1.00
Casserole, 1½ qt., oval, au gratin cover	14.00	Sugar		4.50
Casserole, 2 qt., knob cover	15.00	Sugar cover		5.00
Creamer	5.00	Tumbler, 5 oz., juice		6.00
Cup, 5 oz., snack	3.00	Tumbler, 11 oz., tea		8.00
Cup, 8 oz.	4.00	Tray, 11" x 6", rectangular, snack		4.00
Custard, 6 oz., low or dessert	3.00			

wheat dinnerware

Heat-resistant; golden wheat on a clean contemporary shape.
Matches Wheat ovenware. In open stock and packaged sets.

			Doz. Ctn.	Lbs. Ctn.
W4679/65	8 oz	cup	3	14
W4629/65	5¾"	saucer	3	14
W4674/65	4⅝"	dessert	3	11
W4638/65	7⅜"	salad plate	3	23
W4667/65	6⅝"	soup plate	3	25
W4646/65	10"	dinner plate	3	44
W4678/65	8¼"	vegetable bowl	1	14
W4647/65	12 x 9"	platter	1	20
W4653/65		sugar/cover	1	9
W4654/65		creamer	1	7

Packed Sets

		Sets Ctn.	Lbs. Ctn.
W4600/46	16 pc set, display carton, 4 cups, 4 saucers, 4 desserts, 4 dinner plates	4	38
W4600/47	35 pc set, 6 cups, 6 saucers, 6 desserts, 6 soup plates, 6 dinner plates, vegetable, platter, sugar/cover, creamer	1	23
W4600/48	53 pc set, 8 cups, 8 saucers, 8 desserts, 8 salad plates, 8 soup plates, 8 dinner plates, vegetable, platter, sugar/cover, creamer	1	34

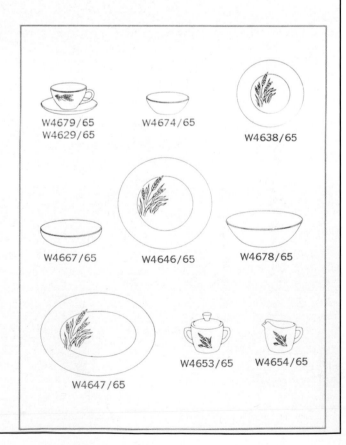

W4679/65
W4629/65

W4674/65

W4638/65

W4667/65

W4646/65

W4678/65

W4647/65

W4653/65

W4654/65

ASHTRAYS

One nationally syndicated writer on collectibles has recommended smoking paraphernalia as one of the future's biggest phenomena. I am not a prophet, but I do know that Fire-King ashtrays are being bought up shortly after being placed on the market. Being a non-smoker, but raised in a tobacco state, Kentucky, I cannot see smokers ever giving up this vice completely, making ashtrays obsolete; but I do believe ashtrays may well make entertaining collections!

Anchor Hocking made an abundance of ashtrays. They are distributed throughout this book in a number of patterns, but I have gathered an assortment to show here.

Pictured here are close-ups of a New York World's Fair, Jonestown Bicentennial, and California souvenir ashtrays. Two are priced in row 5 of page 133. The Jonestown Bicentennial sells for $4.00 to $5.00 nationally, but $8.00 to $12.00 around Jonestown. In California, you might be asked $20.00 for that one that will sell around $10.00 other places. Get the idea? By the way, just lately, we've had buyers inquiring what Bicentennial items we have for sale.

The Anchor Hocking 75 year anniversary ashtray was so loved by we Fire-King people you can see it pictured in both rows 1 and row 5. Obviously, people at the session were adamant we not overlook it.

The 4¼" Jade-ite ashtray is being sought by nearly all Jade-ite Fire-King collectors without success. Those marked Fire-King are uncommon. If you smoke or not, you might consider saving a few of these.

Items

Page 133	Row 1:	#1	Jade-ite, 4¼"	*28.00 – 30.00
		#2	75 years Anchor Hocking Anniversary	20.00 – 22.50
		#3	Royal Ruby, 4¼"	15.00 – 18.00
	Row 2:	#1	Waterford Vitrock, 4"	10.00 – 12.00
		#2	Royal Ruby, 4"	7.00 – 8.00
		#3	Royal Ruby pentagonal, 3¼"	7.00 – 8.00
		#4	Peach Lustre, 3"	7.00 – 8.00
	Row 3:	#1	Ivory "Tulip," 4⁷⁄₁₆"	14.00 – 16.00
		#2	Lustre "Tulip," 4⁷⁄₁₆"	8.00 – 10.00
		#3	Manhattan, "25 years of Progress, Anchor Hocking"	18.00 – 20.00
		#4	Manhattan, "Technical Society, 5th anniversary, 1939"	6.00 – 8.00
	Row 4:	#1	Turquoise Blue set (3½", 4⅝", 5¾") w/gold drizzled design	50.00 – 55.00
		#2	Forest Green set (3½", 4⅝", 5¾")	20.00 – 22.50
		#3	White, 3½"	10.00 – 12.00
		#4	Turquoise Blue set (3½", 4⅝", 5¾")	35.00 – 37.50
	Row 5:	#1,2	Tavares National Bank, White Hall Hotel, 5¼"	5.00 – 6.00
		#3	New York World's Fair, 5¼"	20.00 – 22.50
		#4	75 years Anchor Hocking Anniversary	20.00 – 22.50
		#5	Pink flowers, 4"	6.00 – 8.00
		#6	California, 4"	8.00 – 10.00
	Row 6:	#1	Wexford, 5½"	3.50 – 4.50
		#2,3	Azure-ite Atlantic City, 3½" (add $2.00 for gold)	18.00 – 20.00
		#4	EAPC stand, 6"	10.00 – 12.00
		#5	Crystal American eagle, 4½"	10.00 – 12.00
		#6	Forest Green experimental	80.00 – 100.00
		#7	Cobalt blue, 4⅝"	20.00 – 25.00

*marked $35.00 – 40.00

BOWLS (BATTER, BASKETWEAVE, BON BON, BULB & FLOWER POTS)

Amusing combinations turned up trying to alphabetize this Items section; yet, so be it for simplicity in using the book. The Turquoise Blue and Fruits decorated batter bowls are still most preferred of all Fire-King batter bowls. The crystal one pictured on the bottom of page 135 is not commonly found.

Page 134		#1	Jade-ite, 6½", ruffled rim diamond bottom bowl, bon bon	40.00 –	55.00
Page 135	Row 1:	#1	Azur-ite, 6½", ruffled rim diamond bottom bowl, bon bon	30.00 –	35.00
		#2	Ivory, 6½", ruffled rim diamond bottom bowl, bon bon	35.00 –	40.00
	Row 2:	#1	"Blue and Gold Leaf"	18.00 –	20.00
		#2	Crystal, 2 qt.	12.00 –	15.00
		#3	Fruits	200.00 –	225.00
	Row 3:	#1	Anchorwhite, 1" band	14.00 –	18.00
		#2	Lustre (mint inside and out)	30.00 –	35.00
		#3	Ivory, ¾" band	15.00 –	18.00
	Row 4:	#1	Crystal, tab handled	18.00 –	20.00
		#2	Forest Green, tab handled	20.00 –	25.00
	Row 5:	#1	Jade-ite (¾" band at top)	35.00 –	40.00
			Same (1" band, not pictured)	40.00 –	45.00
		#2	Jade-ite w/Anchor Hocking label	50.00 –	60.00
		#3	Turquoise Blue	350.00 –	400.00
	Row 6:	#1	Crystal batter w/diamonds and panels	30.00 –	35.00
		#2	White with ¾" red band	55.00 –	60.00
Page 136	Row 1:	#1	Forest Green, 6¼", bulb	10.00 –	12.00
		#2	Jade-ite, 6¾", ruffled top bulb	20.00 –	25.00
		#3	Vitrock, 6¼", bulb	10.00 –	12.00
	Row 2:	#1	Jade-ite, 6¼", bulb	18.00 –	20.00
		#2	Crystal, 6¾", ruffled top bulb	12.00 –	14.00
		#3	Fired-on green Vitrock, 6¼", bulb	8.00 –	10.00
	Row 3:	#1	Fired-on green Vitrock, 6½", bon bon	8.00 –	10.00
		#2	Fired-on Peach Vitrock, 10⅝", miniature flower garden tray	12.50 –	15.00
		#3	Fired-on Dusty Rose Vitrock, 6½", bon bon	8.00 –	10.00
	Row 4:	#1	Forest Green, 6½", ruffled rim diamond bottom bowl, bon bon	8.00 –	10.00
		#2	Azur-ite, 6½", ruffled rim diamond bottom bowl, bon bon	30.00 –	35.00
		#3	Jade-ite, 6", straight rim diamond bottom bowl, bon bon	30.00 –	35.00
		#4	Ivory, 6½", ruffled rim diamond bottom bowl, bon bon	25.00 –	30.00
Page 137	Row 1:	#1	Basket Weave, Milk White	7.00 –	8.00
		#2,3,4	Basket Weave, fired-on Blue, Green, or Coral	18.00 –	20.00
		#5	Basket Weave, Turquoise Blue	125.00 –	150.00
	Row 2:	#1	Bulb bowl, 5¼", Jade-ite	20.00 –	25.00
		#2	Cactus pot, 2¼" x 2½", Jade-ite	18.00 –	20.00
		#3,5	Bulb bowl, 5¼", blue or yellow	10.00 –	12.00
		#4	Cactus pot, 2¼" x 2½", blue	18.00 –	20.00
		#6	Cactus pot, 2¼" x 2½", Vitrock	8.00 –	10.00
		#7	Bulb bowl, 5¼", Jade-ite decorated	20.00 –	25.00
	Row 3:	#1	Flower pot, 3⅝", smooth top, Ivory	16.00 –	18.00
		#2	Flower pot, 3⅝", smooth top, Jade-ite	16.00 –	18.00
		#3	Flower pot, 3⅝", smooth top, Azur-ite	16.00 –	18.00
	Row 4:	#1	Flower pot, 3¼", ruffled top, fired-on green	25.00 –	30.00
		#2	Flower pot, 3¼", ruffled top, fired-on blue	15.00 –	18.00
		#3	Flower pot, 3¼", ruffled top, fired-on yellow	15.00 –	18.00
		#4	Flower pot, 3¼", scalloped top, Jade-ite	25.00 –	30.00
	Row 5:	#1	Jardiniere, Hobnail, 4½", Milk White	3.00 –	4.00
		#2	Flower pot, 3¼", ruffled top, Ivory	8.00 –	10.00
		#4	Flower pot, 3¼", ruffled top, Tangerine Red	12.50 –	15.00
		#3	Jardiniere, Hobnail, 5½", Milk White	3.00 –	4.00
		#5	Jardiniere, Hobnail, 4½", Coral	7.00 –	8.00

Items

Items

BOWLS, MIXING (BEADED EDGE, COLONIAL KITCHEN, AND RIBBED)

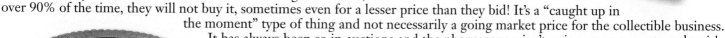

Had I known my book was just a beginning point for prices for some of the mixing bowls pictured, I would have stocked up on more of them. I bought the set of Colonial Rim bowls pictured on page 140 on my way back from Florida to attend the photo shoot for the first book. I promptly sold them for the book price of $125.00. What a difference two years made in prices for Jade-ite. Now they are selling for $275.00. Still, prices have dropped about twenty percent from the frenetically high prices paid about a year ago; most Jade-ite mixing bowl prices have at least doubled from those recorded in the first book.

I had great help from dealers and collectors in pricing the book, but none of us could have foreseen the influence of the Internet. Prices are instantaneous there; and, at first, most prices from electrifying auctions were taken as gospel although they are probably one of the most unreliable sources of **general** pricing known to humanity. If at least two people with money want a particular item at auction, the sky is the limit. Try to sell that same item to the next highest bidder, and over 90% of the time, they will not buy it, sometimes even for a lesser price than they bid! It's a "caught up in the moment" type of thing and not necessarily a going market price for the collectible business. It has always been so in auctions and the phenomenon isn't going away; so, get used to it!

The prices listed in this book represent the thoughts of some serious Fire-King collectors and dealers as well as my own. The 4⅞" Beaded Edge Jade-ite bowl still confuses some dealers and collectors alike. This bowl, the 10 ounce breakfast bowl, and 15 ounce deep bowls are pictured side by side on page 218. Learn the difference and save yourself some money! In any case, you may find a wide variety of prices on mixing bowls; buy those whose prices you feel you can afford.

Pictured are a silver overlay, ribbed "Left-Over" storage jar ($12.00 – 15.00) and a boxed set of the Diamond bowls. Add $25.00 to $30.00 for the box. The smaller ribbed jars with lids were refrigerator storage jars even though they are considered to be mixing bowls by some collectors when found lidless.

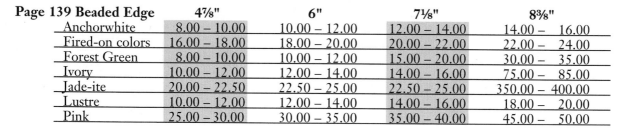

Page 139 Beaded Edge	4⅞"	6"	7⅛"	8⅜"
Anchorwhite	8.00 – 10.00	10.00 – 12.00	12.00 – 14.00	14.00 – 16.00
Fired-on colors	16.00 – 18.00	18.00 – 20.00	20.00 – 22.00	22.00 – 24.00
Forest Green	8.00 – 10.00	10.00 – 12.00	15.00 – 20.00	30.00 – 35.00
Ivory	10.00 – 12.00	12.00 – 14.00	14.00 – 16.00	75.00 – 85.00
Jade-ite	20.00 – 22.50	22.50 – 25.00	22.50 – 25.00	350.00 – 400.00
Lustre	10.00 – 12.00	12.00 – 14.00	14.00 – 16.00	18.00 – 20.00
Pink	25.00 – 30.00	30.00 – 35.00	35.00 – 40.00	45.00 – 50.00

Page 140 Colonial Kitchen	6"	7³⁄₁₆"	8¾"
Anchorwhite	6.00 – 8.00	8.00 – 10.00	10.00 – 12.00
"Blue and Gold Leaf"	unknown	12.50 – 15.00	15.00 – 20.00
Diamonds	60.00 – 70.00	60.00 – 70.00	60.00 – 70.00
Fired-on bands	17.50 – 20.00	20.00 – 25.00	25.00 – 30.00
Fired-on colors (see page 151)	35.00 – 40.00	40.00 – 45.00	45.00 – 50.00
Fruits (see page 198)	12.00 – 14.00	14.00 – 16.00	16.00 – 18.00
Jade-ite	70.00 – 75.00	90.00 – 100.00	90.00 – 100.00
Lustre	12.50 – 15.00	15.00 – 17.50	17.50 – 20.00
Peach Blossom (see page 201)	14.00 – 16.00	16.00 – 18.00	18.00 – 20.00

Page 141 Ribbed	4¾"	5⅜"	6"	7½"	9"
Azur-ite		40.00 – 50.00			
Crystal		6.00 – 8.00			12.00 – 15.00
Fired-on colors		10.00 – 12.50			
Forest Green	8.00 – 10.00		10.00 – 12.50	15.00 – 17.50	
Ivory	18.00 – 20.00			25.00 – 30.00	
Jade-ite	90.00 – 100.00	20.00 – 25.00		25.00 – 30.00	
Vitrock or red stripe		12.00 – 15.00	20.00 – 25.00	20.00 – 25.00	25.00 – 30.00

BOWLS, MIXING (SPLASH PROOF)

Splash Proof bowls are the most abundant of all Anchor Hocking mixing bowls. If you only own one Anchor Hocking mixing bowl, chances are it's a Splash Proof, and more often than not, a two-quart one. Showing every possible Splash Proof mixing bowl would have been redundant and used valuable book space needed for other things. A sampling of all styles of decorated bowls is illustrated and prices are given for those that have been corroborated in collections.

One of the greatest finds in the mixing bowl category was not even decorated. It is a smaller version than the one quart Jade-ite. It is pictured below for comparison to the rarely seen one quart. This new discovery stands 3½" tall and is 5⁹⁄₁₆" in diameter and holds twenty ounces when full. The two-quart Splash Proof at right has been converted to use as an ice bucket with holder and hinged lid.

The red and white flower decorated Jade-ite bowls shown on page 143 are quite rare. Blue "Distlefink" (page 143, row 2) can also be found with red birds (page 151). The Modern Tulip decoration (page 145, row 1) comes in black (center) and navy blue (right), with the navy blue being the rarer color. Kitchen Aids bowls (page 145, row 3 and row 4) are among the most desired mixing bowl sets with the Spag's advertising on the two-quart bowl a high priority on everyone's wish list. Kitchen Aids bowls were even found in blue and yellow decorations last year. Now, find that missing green (?) decoration to add to the set. To any of the mixing bowl set prices, add $25.00 to $35.00 for a box.

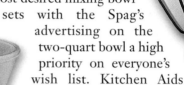

Items

Page 143	6¾" 1 qt.	7⅝" 2 qt.	8½" 3 qt.	9½" 4 qt.
"Distlefink"	150.00 – 200.00	100.00 – 125.00	100.00 – 125.00	100.00 – 125.00
Fired-on colors		14.00 – 16.00		
"Fruits"	55.00 – 75.00	55.00 – 75.00	100.00 – 125.00	100.00 – 125.00
Jade-ite w/decal flowers	400.00 – 450.00	300.00 – 350.00	300.00 – 350.00	300.00 – 350.00
"Outlined Fruit"	100.00 – 125.00	90.00 – 100.00	90.00 – 100.00	90.00 – 100.00

Page 144	6¾" 1 qt.	7⅝" 2 qt.	8½" 3 qt.	9½" 4 qt.
Crystal	20.00 – 22.00	22.00 – 24.00	25.00 – 28.00	28.00 – 30.00
Ivory	18.00 – 20.00	10.00 – 12.00	18.00 – 20.00	20.00 – 22.00
Jade-ite	250.00 – 300.00	60.00 – 65.00	90.00 – 100.00	90.00 – 100.00
Turquoise Blue	18.00 – 20.00	22.00 – 24.00	22.00 – 24.00	
White	18.00 – 20.00	10.00 – 12.00	18.00 – 20.00	20.00 – 22.00

Page 145	6¾" 1 qt.	7⅝" 2 qt.	8½" 3 qt.	9½" 4 qt.
Apples, Tulips on white	30.00 – 35.00	25.00 – 30.00	30.00 – 35.00	35.00 – 40.00
Black Dots	30.00 – 35.00	30.00 – 35.00	30.00 – 35.00	30.00 – 35.00
Kitchen Aids	100.00 – 125.00	*65.00 – 75.00	90.00 – 100.00	90.00 – 100.00
Modern Tulip black	20.00 – 22.50	18.00 – 20.00	18.00 – 20.00	20.00 – 22.50
Modern Tulip navy blue	75.00 – 90.00	65.00 – 75.00	65.00 – 75.00	65.00 – 75.00
Red Dots, Tulips on Ivory	20.00 – 22.50	20.00 – 22.50	25.00 – 27.50	27.50 – 30.00

*Row 3 #1 Spag's – $75.00 – 90.00   Row 3 #3 Spag's Anniversary – $75.00 – 90.00

BOWLS, MIXING (FRED PRESS, 400 LINE, SWEDISH MODERN, SWIRL, UNUSUAL AND NEW ADDITIONS)

Displayed on page 147 are eleven two-quart bowls that were utilized extensively with candle warmers. Candle warmers were misplaced, abused, and tossed out, leaving a myriad of gold decorated, signed Fred Press bowls lacking their warmers!

Swedish Modern style mixing bowls shown on the bottom of page 148 have caught the fancy of more collectors than there are available sets, something that always stimulates prices. Add $2.00 to $5.00 for a label on a mixing bowl and $35.00 to $40.00 to the prices listed for a boxed set. By the way, Swedish Modern's three-piece box is harder to find than the four-piece!

Swirl mixing bowls are readily found except for the 5" size in all colors. Jade-ite 5" bowls have tripled in price in only two years; interestingly, most collectors who have been willing to pay that price already own one or more. On page 150 at the top are an Azur-ite, a translucent green, and a Jade-ite bowl that had the rim turned down making a flanged edge. There is also an Ivory bowl with a red edge applied to match the Sunrise pattern. Row 2 shows a set of Ivory with Anchor Hocking's #253 decoration.

The top of page 151 shows bowls not pictured previously, and all are priced in their respective categories. I might add that the Splash Proof Jade-ite with **decaled** tulips sold for $75.00, nowhere in the range of other floral decorated bowls. The blue Gazelle sells about $40.00, but is plentiful enough not to sell quickly at that.

Page 147 Splash Proof Fred Press

All bowls are 7⅝", 2 qt. splash proof bowls (Fred Press signed except Row 2).	15.00 – 20.00
Row 2 #1 vegetables	30.00 – 35.00
Row 2 #2 gold dots	25.00 – 30.00

Page 148 top, 400 Line

	5"	6"	7¼"	8⅜"
"Granite Ware"	35.00 – 40.00	25.00 – 30.00	30.00 – 35.00	35.00 – 40.00
Dutch Clover	3.00 – 4.00	5.00 – 6.00	6.00 – 8.00	8.00 – 10.00
Bold Colors	5.00 – 6.00	6.00 – 8.00	8.00 – 10.00	10.00 – 12.00

Page 149 bottom, Swedish Modern

	5"	6"	7¼"	8⅜"
Anchorwhite	12.50 – 15.00			
*Jade-ite	50.00 – 55.00	100.00 – 125.00	90.00 – 100.00	90.00 – 125.00
Turquoise Blue	25.00 – 30.00	30.00 – 35.00	30.00 – 35.00	55.00 – 60.00

* add $35.00 – 40.00 for box set

Page 150 Swirl

	5"	6"	7"	8"	9"
Anchorwhite	18.00 – 20.00	4.00 – 5.00	6.00 – 7.50	6.00 – 7.50	10.00 – 12.00
Ivory		6.00 – 7.50	8.00 – 10.00	10.00 – 12.50	12.50 – 15.00
Jade-ite	150.00 – 165.00	25.00 – 28.00	22.50 – 25.00	25.00 – 28.00	28.00 – 30.00
Peach Lustre		7.50 – 10.00	8.00 – 10.00	10.00 – 12.50	12.50 – 15.00
Rainbow		20.00 – 22.00	24.00 – 26.00	24.00 – 26.00	24.00 – 26.00

Page 151 top, Unusual

	6"	7"	8"	9"
Red trim				60.00 – 75.00
Jade-ite flanged rim			90.00 – 100.00	
Jade-ite opalescent	90.00 – 100.00			
Azur-ite		100.00 – 125.00		
Floral decoration #253	40.00 – 50.00	40.00 – 50.00	50.00 – 60.00	50.00 – 60.00

Page 151 bottom

Rainbow box only	35.00 – 40.00

Items

146

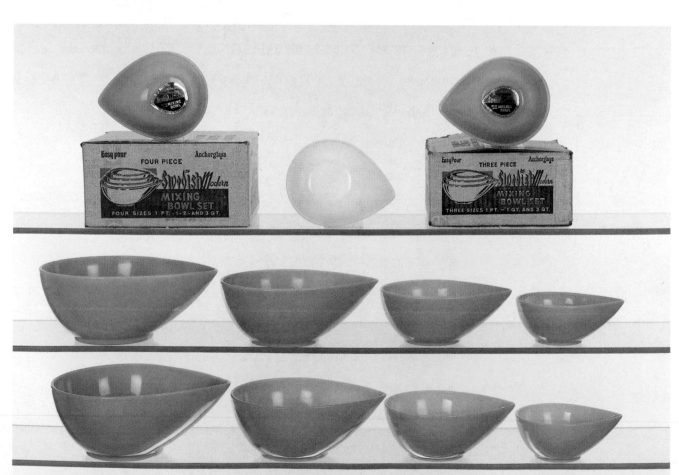

"KITCHEN AIDS" DECORATION

RANGE SET

W300/239—4 Pce. Range Set
  Each Set in Gift Carton, 8 Sets to Shipping Carton — 19 lbs.
COMPOSITION: One Salt Shaker—White Top
        One Pepper Shaker—White Top
        One Range Jar & Cover

The above Range Set and matching Mixing Bowl Sets in "Kitchen Aids" decoration, are not available in Open Stock.

W300/237—3 Pce. Mixing Bowl Set
  Each Set Nested & Packed in an Individual Cell, 8 Sets to Shipping Carton — 44 lbs.
COMPOSITION: One 1 Qt. Mixing Bowl
        One 2 Qt. Mixing Bowl
        One 3 Qt. Mixing Bowl

W300/238—4 Pce. Mixing Bowl Set
  Each Set in Gift Carton, 4 Sets to Shipping Carton — 37 lbs.
COMPOSITION: One 1 Qt. Mixing Bowl
        One 2 Qt. Mixing Bowl
        One 3 Qt. Mixing Bowl
        One 4 Qt. Mixing Bowl

HEAT-PROOF

151

BOWLS AND MUGS (CARTOON, CHARACTER, CHILDREN, DIAMONDS, TRANSPORTATION, AND TULIPS)

Optimistically, the price listing will satisfy any queries. I will add new mugs with each book as there is almost an endless supply. The top two rows of mugs pictured on page 154 were called Patio mugs. See the boxed set on the bottom of that page. Only white seemed to be nationally distributed. The others are found mostly in the upper Midwest. There is another style of Davy Crockett bowl pictured on page 159 which is 5" in diameter.

Items

Page 153	Row 1:	#1,2	Davy Crockett mug, 8 oz., brown or red	18.00 – 20.00
		#3	Forest Green Davy Crockett tumbler	20.00 – 25.00
		#4,5	Robin or Batman mug	18.00 – 20.00
	Row 2:	#1-5	ABC and prayer mugs and bowls	12.50 – 15.00
	Row 3:	#1-5	Circus bowl	20.00 – 22.00
	Row 4:	#1,2	Davy Crockett, 4¾", bowl, red or brown	20.00 – 22.50
		#3,4	Davy Crockett, 4¾", bowl, blue or green	27.50 – 30.00
		#5	Davy Crockett, 4¾", bowl, peach	35.00 – 37.50
	Row 5:	#1	Davy Crockett, 4¾", bowl, black	20.00 – 22.50
		#2-4	Davy Crockett, 4¾", bowl, Woodsman, Statesman, or Hunter	30.00 – 32.50
		#5	Davy Crockett, 4¾", bowl, yellow	42.50 – 45.00
	Row 6:	#1	Yellow cars	12.50 – 15.00
		#2	Davy Crockett shaped bowl, 4¾", rose decorated w/gold	20.00 – 22.50
		#3	Davy Crockett shaped bowl, 4¾", fired-on yellow	18.00 – 20.00
		#4	Davy Crockett shaped bowl, 4¾", Turquoise Blue	90.00 –100.00
		#5	Baby bowl, blue w/crawling baby	25.00 – 30.00
Page 154	Row 1:	#1-5	Patio crystal mugs	20.00 – 25.00
	Row 2:	#1-3	Patio mugs, white w/colored interiors	12.50 – 15.00
		#4,5	Patio mugs, w/Goebel Beer ad (for Patio Pleasure)	30.00 – 35.00
		#6	Patio mug, white	10.00 – 12.50
	Row 3:	#1-3	Disney mugs	10.00 – 12.00
		#4	Jimmy Cricket mug	50.00 – 55.00
		#5-7	Disney mugs	10.00 – 12.00
	Row 4:	#1	Boxed set of 4 Jade-ite mugs	50.00 – 55.00
		#2	Boxed set of 4 Ivory tall 8½" mugs	80.00 – 85.00
	Row 5:	#1	Patio pack; 4 Patio mugs and 4 Patio platters	100.00 –110.00
		#2	Shaving set in box w/one mug	25.00 – 30.00
		#3,4,5	Eagle mug only	10.00 – 12.00
Page 155	Row 1:	#1,2,4	Camelot mugs	4.00 – 5.00
		#3,5	Kimberly mugs	3.00 – 4.00
		#6	Spruce Goose	20.00 – 25.00
		#7	R.M.S. Queen Mary	10.00 – 12.50
	Row 2:	#1-4	Gingham	4.00 – 5.00
		#5	Chicago Cubs	20.00 – 25.00
		#6	Chicago	10.00 – 12.50
		#7	McDonald's (Many Happy Returns)	10.00 – 12.50
	Row 3:	#1-3	Butterflies	5.00 – 6.00
		#4-7	Signed Hildi (mouse, frog, love bugs, caterpillar)	8.00 – 12.00
	Row 4:	#1	Burger Queen	8.00 – 10.00
		#2-4	Super Stripe	3.00 – 4.00
		#5-7	Pop Floral (Rose, Tulip, violet)	5.00 – 6.00
	Row 5:	#1	Bazooka bubble gum	15.00 – 20.00
		#2	A&W	10.00 – 12.00
		#3	Stuckey's coffee club	10.00 – 12.00
		#4-6	Bonanza, Burger Chef, Burger King	8.00 – 10.00
		#7	McDonald's	4.00 – 5.00
	Row 6:	#1	Courtley Shaving mug w/Courtley on front	20.00 – 25.00
		#2	Same with paper top label	25.00 – 30.00
		#3	Christmas mug	20.00 – 25.00
	Row 7:	#1	Chili bowl	12.50 – 15.00
		#2	Coffee mug	8.00 – 10.00
		#3,4	Lone Ranger Vitrock cup (2 views)	35.00 – 40.00
	Top right:		Tulsa Experimental Aircraft Association	15.00 – 20.00
	Middle right:		Honeymoon Hideaway	6.00 – 8.00

Items

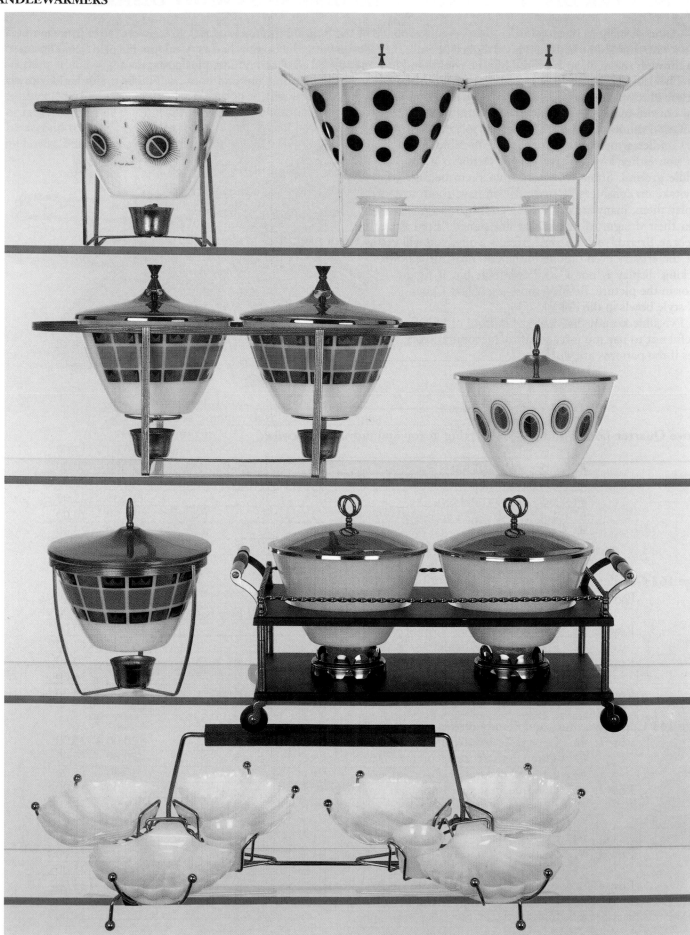

Items

CANDY AND DESSERT DISHES, CIGARETTE AND POWDER JARS

Anchor Hocking classified the Vitrock boxes at the bottom of the next page as Jewel boxes. All Jade-ite pieces in the categories on these pages have increased in price dramatically. On page 166, notice that the edges of the "Party Dessert" bowl flare out and those of the liner plate are rounded; in the "Leaf and Blossom" bowl, edges do not flare and the edges of the liner plate are pointed! The yellow label below is from a Forest Green, Maple Leaf dessert bowl.

Below Maple Leaf and Sea Shell candy or dessert dishes

Row 1:	#1,2	Royal Ruby or Forest Green Maple Leaf (add $7.00 for label)	10.00 – 12.50
	#3	George Briard decorated Sea Shell w/tongs	15.00 – 20.00
	#4	Jade-ite Maple Leaf (add $10.00 for cooking spoon label	25.00 – 28.00
Row 2:	#1,2	Lustre or Forest Green Sea Shell	8.00 – 10.00
	#3	White Sea Shell	6.00 – 8.00
	#4	Jade-ite Sea Shell (add $8.00 for desserts label)	24.00 – 27.00

Page 165 Candy, cigarette, and powder jars

Row 1:	#1	Crystal, 6" comport	10.00 – 12.00
	#2	Crystal, satinized, 6¾" candy and cover	20.00 – 25.00
	#3	Aquamarine, 6¾" candy and cover	40.00 – 50.00
	#4	Forest Green comport, 6½"	50.00 – 55.00
Row 2:	#1	Jade-ite, 6¾" candy and cover (**mint lid**)	90.00 – 95.00
	#2	Jade-ite, 6" comport	90.00 – 95.00
	#3	Ivory, 6" comport	12.50 – 15.00
	#4	White, 6¾" candy and cover	15.00 – 17.50
Row 3:	American Artware Line		
	#1,2,4,5	Dusty Rose or Spring Green puff box w/Ivory (Vitrock) cover	25.00 – 27.50
	#3	Ivory (Vitrock) jewel box w/cover	27.50 – 30.00
Row 4:	American Artware Line		
	#1–4	Dusty Rose or Spring Green jewel box w/Ivory (Vitrock) cover	25.00 – 27.50
	#5	Jade-ite jewel box w/cover	75.00 – 85.00
Row 5:	#1,2	Jade-ite jewel box w/cover, hand decorated	85.00 – 95.00

Page 166 Dessert sets and lamps

Row 1:	#1,3	7" hurricane lamp with globe	45.00 – 50.00
	#2	Crystal Leaf and Blossom set	15.00 – 17.50
Row 2:	#1	Peach Lustre "Party Dessert" set	10.00 – 12.00
	#2	Azur-ite bowl, 5¼"	12.50 – 15.00
	#3	Ivory "Party Dessert" set	25.00 – 27.50
Row 3:	#1	Blue Leaf and Blossom set	12.50 – 15.00
	#2	Forest Green Leaf and Blossom set	18.00 – 20.00
	#3	Jade-ite Leaf and Blossom set	30.00 – 35.00
Row 4:	#1,2,3	Green, yellow or Peach Leaf and Blossom set	12.50 – 15.00

Items

Items

CHILDREN'S DISHES

Collectors of children's dishes now have a new piece to add to their quest. Pictured below, on the right is a saucer that goes with the "Kiddie Mealtime Set" shown in row 3 on page 168. Since the set consisted of a mug, bowl, and plate, the saucer becomes a mystery item. Was there a cup or was the saucer supposed to go with the mug? I bet there is an undiscovered cup lurking out there. However, the boxed set says "3 pce.," and they are accounted for already.

Fire-King children's dishes play only a small role in the whole realm of collecting children's dishwares. All pieces pictured on page 168 are Fire-King or its Ivory forerunner, Vitrock.

Row 2 consists of children's divided plates (7½") and a Jade-ite child's mug. Three different colored trims and Jade-ite are the only varieties known. I bought the Jade-ite plate pictured here for $150.00 for one of the people who helped with the first book. We couldn't find anyone who helped in pricing the book who thought it was worth more than $100.00; however, I listed it at the $150.00 that had been paid. Here, I need to relate a story I heard about from the Internet. One of these plates went online for auction; the mass bidding stopped around $250.00 except for two people who wanted it. At the very last minute, it sold for $1,724.00! Two more of these have been offered for auction and the highest bid has been in the $400.00 range which did not reach the reserve placed on them. This is a prime example why auction prices sometimes mean very little in the **real** world. I cannot list it for that astronomical amount. One sale is not a "trend." It would have to continue in that range first.

Row 4 contains a "Snow White and the Seven Dwarfs" bowl. Two additional views are shown below, still not revealing all the pictures! It was a General Mills premium beginning February 9, 1953; these moulds were scrapped March 14, 1957, according to Anchor Hocking records.

Page 168	Row 1:	#1	"Little Bo Peep," 7¾" divided plate, red on Vitrock	28.00 – 30.00
		#2	"Little Bo Peep," mug, red on Vitrock	12.00 – 14.00
		#3,5	"Little Bo Peep," 7¾" divided plate, multicolored or blue on Vitrock	32.50 – 35.00
		#4,6	"Little Bo Peep," mug, multicolored or blue on Vitrock	16.00 – 18.00
	Row 2:	#1	Jade-ite, 7½", divided plate	400.00 – 500.00
		#2	Jade-ite, child's mug (same mould as Bo-Peep)	200.00 – 250.00
		#3	Pink-trimmed Ivory, 7½", divided plate	45.00 – 50.00
		#4	Blue-trimmed Ivory, 7½", divided plate	45.00 – 50.00
		#5	Turquoise-trimmed Ivory, 7½", divided plate	55.00 – 60.00
	Row 3:	#1	"Bosco" mug	40.00 – 45.00
		#2	Baby decaled bowl	morgue
		#3	Boxed "Kiddie Mealtime Set"	100.00 – 125.00
		#4	"Kiddie Mealtime" mug	20.00 – 25.00
		#5	"Kiddie Mealtime" bowl, 7 oz.	35.00 – 40.00
		#6	"Kiddie Mealtime" plate, 7¼"	15.00 – 20.00
	Row 4:	#1	"Little Bo Peep" bowl, red on Vitrock	30.00 – 40.00
		#2	Coach scene, Vitrock mug	25.00 – 30.00
		#3	Boxed child's bowl w/fork, spoon, and suction cup to hold bowl	40.00 – 50.00
			Bowl only "eat, sleep, play"	27.50 – 30.00
		#4	General Mills "Snow White and Seven Dwarfs" bowl	30.00 – 40.00
		#5	Boxed set Binky's nip cap, measuring pitcher and spoons w/funnel	275.00 – 325.00

Items

167

⚓ PITCHERS OR BALL JUGS

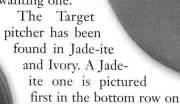

The two newest discoveries in Anchor Hocking ball jugs are pictured here. The Manhattan jug came from Ohio to a show in Michigan where I bought it specifically for the book. It was photographed in November of 1998. Because it crosses the boundaries of Fire-King and Depression glass, I considered it quite a find! The last listing I see for the Manhattan pitcher is in a 1942 catalog, but Jade-ite was supposedly not made until 1946. That probably makes this an experimental piece of Jade-ite. I'm told by workers that these runs were usually about 50 pieces, but not always. I expect another one or two will turn up; so, be on the lookout!* I received a homemade Christmas card showing someone holding this one taken at the '98 Tulsa show where I had it displayed. A couple of the Puro pitchers were found last year, but that's certainly not enough to suit all the collectors wanting one.

The Target pitcher has been found in Jade-ite and Ivory. A Jade-ite one is pictured first in the bottom row on page 171. If you have one of these in Ivory, could we make arrangements to show that one in the next edition? The plain Jade-ite is next in that row and the Swirl is last. The only commonly found Jade-ite pitcher is the plain ball jug; but demand has raised the price on that one quite a bit. This is a fine example of a piece of glass being hard to find, but demand pushing the price way past normal boundaries. **Demand** drives price, often more than rarity!

The first Ivory pitcher in row 3 is vertical ribbed, which Anchor Hocking called Pillar Optic; the next is Manhattan; and the last is Swirl. A plain Ivory ball jug has never been seen as far as I can find out. That does not mean there isn't one to be unearthed.

Those crystal pitchers shown are not presently as desirable as the colored ones, but only the crystal Target could be considered easy to acquire! Royal Ruby Swirl pitchers abound, as does the Royal Ruby ball jug (not pictured). I appreciate your trying to keep me informed of what you find!

Page 170		#1	Jade-ite, Manhattan	2,000.00 – 3,000.00
		#2	Jade-ite Puro	1,000.00 – 1,250.00
Page 171	Row 1:	#1	Crystal, Target line tumbler, 13 oz., iced tea	12.50 – 15.00
		#2	Crystal, Target line ball pitcher, 80 oz.	30.00 – 35.00
		#3	Crystal, Target line tumbler, 9½ oz., water	10.00 – 12.00
	Row 2:	#1	Crystal, vertical ribbed Pillar Optic pitcher	30.00 – 35.00
		#2	Royal Ruby, Swirl ball pitcher, 80 oz.	45.00 – 50.00
			Royal Ruby, ball pitcher, 80 oz. (not pictured)	35.00 – 45.00
		#3	Crystal, Swirl ball pitcher, 80 oz.	30.00 – 35.00
	Row 3:	#1	Ivory, vertical ribbed Pillar Optic pitcher	750.00 – 850.00
		#2	Ivory, Manhattan ball pitcher, 80 oz.	750.00 – 850.00
		#3	Ivory, Swirl ball pitcher, 80 oz.	750.00 – 850.00
	Row 4:	#1	Jade-ite, Target line ball pitcher, 80 oz.	1,250.00 – 1,500.00
			Ivory, Target line ball pitcher, 80 oz. (not pictured)	750.00 – 800.00
		#2	Jade-ite ball pitcher, 80 oz	500.00 – 600.00
		#3	Jade-ite, Swirl ball pitcher, 80 oz.	1,250.00 – 1,500.00

* Today, I received an auction list from Ohio where another Jade-ite Manhattan ball jug is being auctioned in early February. That makes my prediction written a few weeks ago look pretty good.

Items

RANGE SETS (GREASE JARS AND SHAKERS)

The grease jar with matching shakers has become highly collectible. Prices have risen and mint condition screw-on lids are being sold for as much as the complete shakers used to sell. See page 223 for a view of what **mint** shaker tops actually look like as compared to ones that are not. Mint lithographed scripted **(P)** pepper lids will fetch $10.00 – 12.00 and **(S)** salt $12.00 – 15.00. Tulip pepper lids bring $12.00 – 15.00, but salt lids easily bring $18.00 – 20.00, if **mint**. Mint is white background and not beige! Kitchen Aids is the most desirable set to own; that boxed set at right should make a few collectors salivate. Add $50.00 to $75.00 for the Kitchen Aids box and $25.00 – 35.00 for other grease sets or mixing bowl boxes.

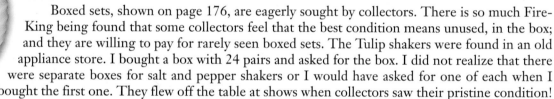

Vitrock grease sets were promoted side by side with Fire-King in both the 1941 and 1942 Anchor Hocking catalogs. The green jar at left is the only one of that color I have seen.

Boxed sets, shown on page 176, are eagerly sought by collectors. There is so much Fire-King being found that some collectors feel that the best condition means unused, in the box; and they are willing to pay for rarely seen boxed sets. The Tulip shakers were found in an old appliance store. I bought a box with 24 pairs and asked for the box. I did not realize that there were separate boxes for salt and pepper shakers or I would have asked for one of each when I bought the first one. They flew off the table at shows when collectors saw their pristine condition!

Items

Page 173 Grease jars

Row	#	Description	Price
Row 1:	#1	Modern Tulips, black	30.00 – 35.00
	#1A	Modern Tulips, navy blue (not pictured)	70.00 – 75.00
	#2	Ivory	16.00 – 18.00
	#3	Crystal with etched design	16.00 – 18.00
	#4	Gold dots on satinized crystal	16.00 – 18.00
Row 2:	#1	Kitchen Aids	150.00 – 175.00
	#2	Crystal	10.00 – 12.00
	#3	Crystal with etched design	16.00 – 18.00
	#4	Tulips on White	30.00 – 35.00
	#4A	Tulips on Ivory	25.00 – 30.00
Row 3:	#1	Black Dots	40.00 – 45.00
	#2	Crystal with cut dots design	16.00 – 18.00
	#3	Crystal with etched design	16.00 – 18.00
	#4	Red Dots on White	40.00 – 45.00
	#4A	Red Dots on Ivory	25.00 – 30.00
Row 4:	#1	Stripes	30.00 – 35.00
	#2	Jade-ite, screw-on lid	75.00 – 85.00
	#3	Crystal, screw-on lid	18.00 – 20.00
	#4	Ivory, screw-on lid	30.00 – 35.00
	#5	Apples	30.00 – 35.00

Page 174 Shakers

Row	#	Description	Price
Row 1:	#1	Modern Tulips, navy blue, pr.	50.00 – 55.00
	#2	Modern Tulips, black, pr.	35.00 – 40.00
	#3,4	Kitchen Aids, pr.	175.00 – 200.00
	#5	Tulips, White, pr.	75.00 – 85.00
	#6	Tulips, Ivory, pr.	65.00 – 75.00
	#7,8	Stripes, pr.	35.00 – 40.00
Row 2:	#1,2	Ivory, pr	14.00 – 16.00
	#3	Primrose, pr.	250.00 – 300.00
	#4	Red Dots on White, pr.	40.00 – 45.00
	#4A	Red Dots on Ivory, pr.	35.00 – 40.00
	#5,6	White, pr.	25.00 – 30.00

Row	#	Description	Price
	#7,8	Black Dots, pr.	50.00 – 60.00
Row 3:	#1-6	Fired-on green, Coral or blue, pr.	15.00 – 18.00
	#7,8	Jade-ite, pr.	80.00 – 90.00
Row 4:	#1	Box set of Philco giveaway shakers	35.00 – 40.00
	#2,3	Crystal horizontal ribbed, pr.	10.00 – 12.00
	#4,5	Crystal w/red dots, pr.	14.00 – 16.00
	#6,7	Soreno, Honey gold, pr.	4.00 – 5.00
	#8	Wexford, crystal, pr.	2.50 – 3.00
	#9,10	Fired-on red, pr.	20.00 – 22.00

Page 175 Vitrock Range Sets

Row	#	Description	Price
Row 1:		"Blue Circle w/Flowers"	
	#1,2	Salt or Pepper	17.50 – 20.00
	#3	Grease jar	30.00 – 35.00
	#4,5	Sugar or Flour	22.50 – 25.00
Row 2:		"Black Circle w/Flowers"	
	#1,2	Salt or Pepper	20.00 – 22.50
	#3	Grease jar	35.00 – 40.00
	#4,5	Sugar or Flour	22.50 – 25.00
Row 3:		"Red Circle w/Flowers"	
	#1,2	Salt or Pepper	17.50 – 20.00
	#3	Grease jar	30.00 – 35.00
	#4,5	Sugar or Flour	22.50 - 25.00
Row 4:		"Red Tulips"	
	#1,2	Salt or Pepper	15.00 – 17.50
	#3	Grease jar	25.00 – 30.00
	#4,5	Sugar or Flour	20.00 – 22.50
Row 5:		"Red Flower Pots"	
	#1,2	Salt or Pepper	15.00 – 17.50
	#3	Grease jar	25.00 – 30.00
	#4,5	Sugar or Flour	20.00 – 22.50
Row 6:		"Green Flower Pots"	
	#1,2	Salt or Pepper	20.00 – 22.50
	#3	Grease jar	37.50 – 40.00
	#4,5	Sugar or Flour	22.50 – 25.00

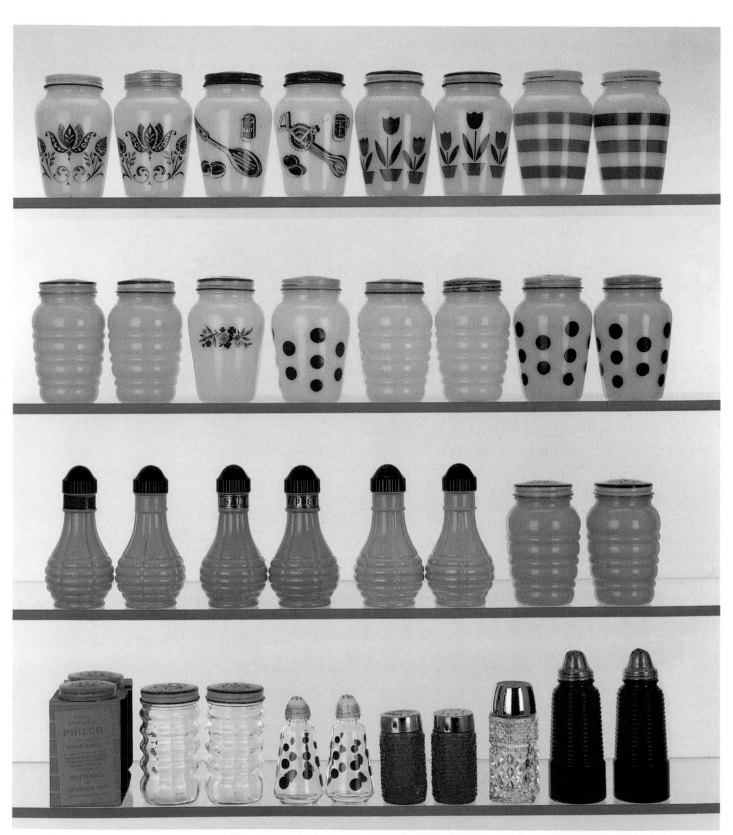

Items

RELISH TRAYS, EGG PLATES, AND REFRIGERATOR CONTAINERS

Most relish trays and egg plates are ignored as items to collect by themselves; however, collectors of each particular color usually pick up an egg plate to match their set. I should point out the Aurora Shell egg plate is pictured at the bottom of page 98 since it is not shown here. It is rarely seen and sells in the $75.00 - 100.00 range. Even if you do not look for egg plates, you need to be aware that several are in high demand. The pink trimmed one atop page 179 ranks way up there in the pecking order.

Egg plates or relish dishes with decaled patterns are being grabbed by collectors of those patterns. Decaled relishes command at least $50.00, and egg plates $100.00, depending upon the pattern.

Admittedly, some of these are difficult to acquire; if more collectors begin to buy them, the prices could skyrocket! Many of the egg plates and relish trays were sold as boxed giftware items. These boxes are sometimes found today, but they only add $4.00 – 5.00 to the price of the item.

Refrigerator containers are not high on most collector want lists at present; so, now might be a good time to store some away. Notice the "Maple Leaf" items in row 2 of page 180. This design is found on both Federal and Anchor Hocking wares. For example, the batter bowl pictured is Federal. If you like this pattern, buy both companies' wares. Federal pieces will be less expensive and will help balance buying Fire-King items. This "Maple Leaf" pattern and the "Blue and Gold Leaf" are predominately found in the Midwest with the St. Louis area having an abundance of both!

Page 178 Relish Trays

Row	#	Description	Price
Row 1:	#1	Honeysuckle, 9¾", three-part, round	90.00 – 100.00
	#2	Turquoise Blue, 22K trimmed, 11⅛", three-part, oblong	10.00 – 12.00
Row 2:	#1	Gift box for round relish	3.00 – 4.00
	#2	Milk White w/Copper trim, 9¾", three-part, round	10.00 – 12.00
	#3	Milk White w/22K gold trim, 9¾", three-part, round	8.00 – 10.00
Row 3:	#1	Lustre, 9¾", three-part, round (mint Lustre on both sides)	14.00 – 16.00
	#2	Milk White, 11⅛", three-part, oblong	6.00 – 8.00
	#3	Gift box for oblong relish	3.00 – 4.00

Page 179 Egg Plates

Row	#	Description	Price
Row 1:	#1	Pink trimmed, 9¾"	100.00 – 125.00
Row 2:	#1	Gift box for egg plate	3.00 – 4.00
	#2	Turquoise Blue, 22K trimmed w/label	22.50 – 25.00
		Same without label	16.00 – 18.00
	#3	Ivory w/22K gold trim	10.00 – 12.00
Row 3:	#1	Milk White w/22K gold trim	8.00 – 10.00
	#2	Turquoise Blue to show reverse side design	16.00 – 18.00
	#3	Lustre (mint)	22.50 – 25.00

Page 180 Refrigerator Containers (crystal lids unless noted)

Row	#	Description	Price
Row 1:	#1	Crystal, 4" x 8"	6.00 – 8.00
	#2	Crystal, 4" x 4"	5.00 – 6.00
	#3	Ivory w/gold band, 4" x 4"	6.00 – 8.00
	#4	Ivory w/gold leaf, 4" x 4"	6.00 – 8.00
	#5	Lustre, 4" x 4"	8.00 – 10.00
	#6	Fruit and flower decal, 4" x 4"	8.00 – 10.00
	#7	Fruit and flower decal, 4" x 8"	15.00 – 18.00
Row 2:	#1	Jade-ite, 4" x 4"	30.00 – 35.00
	#2	Jade-ite, 4" x 8"	45.00 – 50.00
		Jade-ite, 5⅛" x 9½", ribbed (see page 222)	40.00 – 45.00
	#3	"Maple Leaf" FEDERAL GLASS batter bowl	15.00 – 20.00
	#4	"Maple Leaf," 4" x 8"	14.00 – 16.00
	#5	"Maple Leaf," 4" x 4"	8.00 – 10.00
Row 3:	#1	Ivory, 4" x 8"	18.00 – 20.00
	#1A	White (not pictured)	10.00 – 12.00
	#2	Ivory, 4" x 4"	10.00 – 12.00
	#2A	White (not pictured)	5.00 – 6.00
	#3	Milk White, 4¼" x 9", oval	22.50 – 25.00
	#4	Milk White, 4¼", round	18.00 – 20.00
	#5	"Blue and Gold Leaf," 4" x 8", with blue lid	18.00 – 20.00
		"Blue and Gold Leaf," 4" x 8", with white lid	10.00 – 12.00
	#6	"Blue and Gold Leaf," 4" x 4", with blue lid	10.00 – 12.00
		"Blue and Gold Leaf," 4" x 4", with white lid	5.00 – 6.00

Items

Items

Items

VASES

The 5¼" vases shown below were called Table Vases in Anchor Hocking catalogs, but collectors call them "Deco" vases. The fired-on yellow over Vitrock is rarely found, but a crystal satinized one might even be more rarely seen. There again, collector demand makes the yellow on Vitrock more desirable. Yellow on crystal will only sell for half that. The orange colored vase was listed as Tangerine by Anchor Hocking.

Anchor Hocking vases are found in many sizes, shapes, and colors. For the most part, collectors buy vases that go with the colors they collect or ones with eye appeal. They are, also, accoutrements for today's decor.

Below 5¼" Table Vases ("Deco")

All vases crystal fired-on or fired-on Vitrock are priced $8.00 – 10.00 except the following:

Blue or fired-on blue on Vitrock	12.00 – 14.00
Crystal satinized	15.00 – 18.00
Jade-ite (2 shades)	20.00 – 22.50
Tangerine (orange) fired-on Vitrock	10.00 – 12.00
Vitrock	12.50 – 15.00
Yellow fired-on Vitrock	30.00 – 35.00

Page 182 Ivory, Jade-ite, and Vitrock

Row 1:	#1	Vitrock, vertical ribbed, 4" flower pot	4.00 – 5.00
	#2	Vitrock flower pot saucer	6.00 – 8.00
	#3	Ivory 6" flower bowl	10.00 – 12.00
	#4	Ivory, three bands, 4" flower pot	10.00 – 12.00
Row 2:	#1	Vitrock, 7¾", tab handled	15.00 – 18.00
	#2	Jade-ite, 7¾", tab handled	85.00 – 90.00
	#3	Ivory, 7¾", tab handled	12.00 – 15.00
Row 3:	#1,4	Fired-on Tangerine or Green	15.00 – 18.00
	#2,3	Fired-on Blue or Yellow	20.00 – 22.50

Page 183 Tall and Bulbous

Row 1:	#1	Fired-on Green, 9", "Pineapple"	25.00 – 30.00
	#2	Fired-on Coral, 9½", Hobnail	12.50 – 15.00
	#3	Forest Green, 9", "Pineapple"	15.00 – 20.00
	#4	Royal Ruby, 9", "Pineapple"	15.00 – 20.00
Row 2:	#1,6	Green EAPC "look alike"	25.00 – 30.00
	#2,5	Red and yellow flower pots	5.00 – 7.00
	#3	Crystal ball vase w/Apple Blossom	10.00 – 12.00
	#4	Forest Green decorated ball vase	12.00 – 14.00
	#5	Ivory, ribbed, 7¼"	25.00 – 30.00
Row 3:	#1,7	Crystal, 9", "Pineapple"	8.00 – 10.00
	#2	Soreno, 7", crystal	10.00 – 12.00
	#3	Pink, 9", "Pineapple"	22.50 – 25.00
	#4	Yellow, 3¾" w/Niagara Falls	20.00 – 25.00
	#5	Fired-on Blue, 9", "Pineapple"	20.00 – 25.00
	#6	Wexford, 6" bud	3.00 – 4.00

Ovenware

"BLUE HEAVEN" 1970s

Colors: Anchorwhite w/decal

I am starting out the Ovenware section this time with a new pattern, "Blue Heaven." The name "Blue Heaven" was being used by collectors before I even knew this pattern was made by Anchor Hocking. If anyone should have more pertinent information, please let me know. As with many of the ovenware lines, there is a limited amount being found mint. In the past, if you liked this pattern, you bought it and used it. Many pieces I see are heavily worn.

Try to buy only mint pieces unless you, too, are going to use it. It will go in the microwave, but it does tend to heat up; so, do not use it that way regularly or put it down on a cold surface when it comes out of the microwave.

The three-piece set of mixing bowls have tab handles that doubled as pouring spouts. I suspect that could get messy.

	White w/decal
Bowl, 5", chili	8.00 – 10.00
Bowl, mixing, 1 qt.	12.50 – 15.00
Bowl, mixing, 1½ qt.	18.00 – 20.00
Bowl, mixing, 2½ qt.	18.00 – 20.00
Cake pan, 8", square	9.00 – 10.00
Cake pan, 8", round	9.00 – 10.00
Casserole, 12 oz., hdld.	12.50 – 15.00
Casserole, 1 pt.	10.00 – 12.00
Casserole, 1 qt., w/crystal knob cover	10.00 – 12.00
Casserole, 1½ qt., oval w/au gratin cover	20.00 – 22.50
Casserole, 1½ qt., w/crystal knob cover	18.00 – 20.00
Casserole, 2 qt., w/crystal knob cover	20.00 – 22.50
Custard, 6 oz.	3.00 – 4.00
Loaf pan, deep, 5" x 9"	8.00 – 10.00
Mug, 8 oz.	8.00 – 10.00
Utility dish, 6½" x 10½"	6.00 – 8.00

CANDLEGLOW 1967 – 1972

Colors: Anchorwhite w/decal

Candleglow (all one word) is another Anchor Hocking ovenware pattern that is finding favor with only a few avid collectors right now. Ovenware (only) patterns do not attract the buying public as well as those that cross over into dinnerware lines such as Primrose or Meadow Green. In 1967, Candleglow was advertised with free replacement of any pieces broken (with proper use). In 1969, Candleglow was advertised as Lifetime Ovenware! The pattern was discontinued in 1972.

All catalog listings from 1967 to 1972 show the 12 ounce, handled French casserole; however, the label below (taken from one of these casseroles) states it is a Candle Glow (two words) "Custard Cup!" Not only a custard cup instead of French casserole, but the name is now two words! These are more of those discrepancies we find from time to time.

I get letters all the time regarding wrong measurements that were duplicated directly from company catalogs. Today's collectors expect accuracy in books... which are often dependent upon inconsistent sources!

Add $25.00 – 30.00 for a box holding the mixing bowl set.

	White w/decal
Bowl, 5", cereal, 8 oz.	3.00 – 4.00
Bowl, mixing, 1 qt.	8.00 – 10.00
Bowl, mixing, 1½ qt.	10.00 – 12.00
Bowl, mixing, 2½ qt.	12.00 – 14.00
Cake dish, 8", square	6.00 – 7.00
Cake dish, 9", round	6.50 – 7.50
Casserole, 12 oz., hdld.	3.50 – 4.50
Casserole, 1 pt.	8.00 – 10.00
Casserole, 1 qt., w/white cover	8.00 – 9.00

	White w/decal
Casserole, 1½ qt., w/white cover	9.00 – 10.00
Casserole, 1½ qt., oval w/white cover	9.00 – 10.00
Casserole, 2 qt., w/white cover	11.00 – 12.00
Casserole, 3 qt., w/white cover	14.00 – 16.00
Custard, 6 oz.	1.50 – 2.00
Loaf pan, 5" x 9"	6.50 – 7.50
Mug, 8 oz., stacking	5.00 – 6.00
Utility dish, 1½ qt.	5.00 – 6.00
Utility dish, 2 qt.	10.00 – 12.00

Ovenware

CHANTICLEER OR COUNTRY KITCHEN 1965 – 1967

Colors: Anchorwhite w/decal

Chanticleer was introduced in 1965; but in the 1966 catalog, the name was changed to Country Kitchen. Personally, Chanticleer seems apropos with that haughty, puffed-up rooster staring out from each piece. The mug seems hard to find; but unless more collectors start gathering Chanticleer, it will remain difficult to tell how rare some of the pieces might be! Add $25.00 to $30.00 for a box for any Chanticleer pieces.

Ovenware

	White w/decal
Bowl, 5", chili	8.00 – 10.00
Bowl, mixing, 1 qt.	12.50 – 15.00
Bowl, mixing, 1½ qt.	18.00 – 20.00
Bowl, mixing, 2½ qt.	18.00 – 20.00
Bowl, mixing, 3½ qt.	22.50 – 25.00
Cake pan, 8", square	9.00 – 10.00
Cake pan, 8", round	9.00 – 10.00
Casserole, 12 oz., hdld.	12.50 – 15.00
Casserole, 1 pt.	10.00 – 12.00
Casserole, 1 qt., w/crystal knob cover	10.00 – 12.00

	White w/decal
Casserole, 1½ qt., oval w/au gratin cover	20.00 – 22.50
Casserole, 1½ qt., w/crystal knob cover	18.00 – 20.00
Casserole, 2 qt., w/crystal knob cover	20.00 – 22.50
Cup, snack	12.00 – 15.00
Custard, 6 oz.	3.00 – 4.00
Loaf pan, deep, 5" x 9"	8.00 – 10.00
Mug, 8 oz.	18.00 – 20.00
Utility dish, 6½" x 10½"	6.00 – 8.00
Utility dish, 8" x 12½"	20.00 – 22.00

Colors: Copper-Tint (Lustre)

Copper-Tint was a color comparable to the metallic-like Peach Lustre used earlier by Anchor Hocking. The associated troubles of deterioration and rubbing off that besieged Peach Lustre carried on with Copper-Tint. Being used in the oven as it was, baked on goods required elbow grease and this color did not hold up well when scrubbed thoroughly.

Boxed sets of Copper-Tint are available. It's less than 30 years old; and many attics, garages, and basements are yielding sets that were never used. Add $5.00 to 10.00 for a box.

Hopefully, some of these "found" sets will yield information on some of the patterns that have gaps in their history.

A front and back view are shown below of the Mother's Oats box which contained Copper-Tint "Danish Swirl" inside. This box sells for $25.00 – 30.00 and even more, if unopened. No information has been forthcoming on the 10-piece "Sierra Ware" Baking Set. I cannot find one reference to "Sierra Ware" in any catalog I have.

	Copper-Tint
Baker, 1½ qt., no cover	5.00 – 6.50
Baking pan and cover, 5" x 9"	9.00 – 10.00
Cake pan, 8", square	6.00 – 7.00
Cake pan, 8", round	6.00 – 7.00
Casserole, 10 oz., "Danish Swirl"	6.00 – 7.00
Casserole, 12 oz., hdld. w/cover	4.00 – 5.00
Casserole, 1 pt., w/crystal or white cover	6.00 – 7.00
Casserole, 1 qt., w/crystal or white cover	7.00 – 8.00
Casserole, 1½ qt., w/crystal or white cover	7.00 – 8.00
Casserole, 1½ qt., oval w/au gratin cover	9.00 – 10.00
Casserole, 2 qt., w/crystal or white cover	9.00 – 10.00
Custard, 6 oz., plain or scalloped rim	2.00 – 3.00
Custard, 6 oz., "Danish Swirl"	3.00 – 4.00
Dish, 11¾", oval, divided	5.00 – 6.00
Loaf pan, 5" x 9"	7.00 – 8.00
Pie, 5⅜", individual, "Danish Swirl"	4.00 – 5.00
Pie pan, 9"	4.00 – 5.00
Pie pan, 10"	5.00 – 6.00
Utility dish, 6½" x 10½"	5.00 – 6.00
Utility dish, 8" x 12½"	6.00 – 7.00

Ovenware

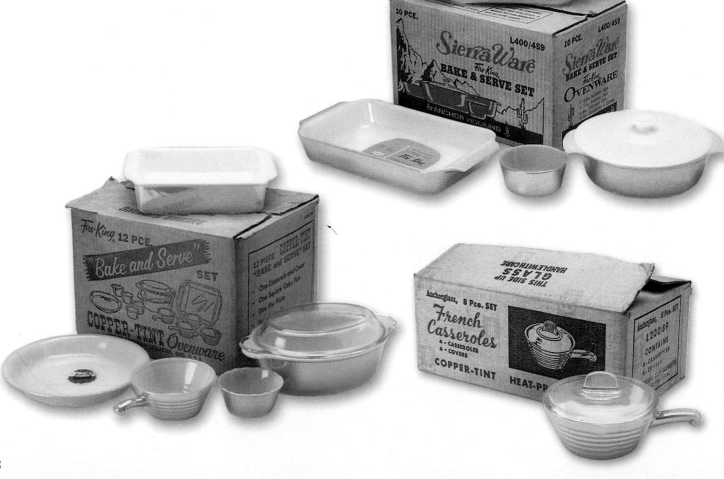

CRYSTAL 1947 – 1992

The 50th Anniversary 9" pie plate and the 16 ounce measuring cup were produced in 1992 to commemorate 50 years of Fire-King. That's "antique" status for glass!

Few collectors seem to be buying crystal Fire-King ovenware at present. I am listing crystal found in the catalogs. On page 190 are representative samples and some boxed sets. Add $1.00 to 3.00 for labels and $5.00 to $15.00 for boxes themselves. There are a couple of catalog pages of crystal in the first book. There is a whole line of Pillsbury items; they are recent vintage.

Below	
50th Anniversary 9" pie plate	12.50 – 15.00
50th Anniversary 16 oz. measuring cup	15.00 – 18.00
Spags, 2 cup	75.00 – 80.00
Spags, 1 cup	85.00 – 90.00
Baker, 8 oz., no cover	2.00 – 3.00
Baker, 1 qt., no cover	2.50 – 3.50
Baker, 1½ qt., no cover	2.50 – 3.50
Baker, 2 qt., no cover	3.00 – 4.00
Baking pan and cover, 5" x 9"	8.00 – 9.00
Baking pan, square, 6¼" x 7¼"	5.00 – 6.00
Cake pan, 8", round	6.00 – 7.00
Cake pan, 8", square	6.00 – 7.00
Casserole, 8 oz., w/crystal knob cover	3.00 – 4.00
Casserole, 1 pt., w/crystal knob cover	3.00 – 4.00
Casserole, 1 qt., w/crystal knob cover	4.00 – 5.00
Casserole, 1½ qt., w/crystal knob cover	5.00 – 6.00
Casserole, 1½ qt., w/utility cover	5.00 – 6.00
Casserole, 1½ qt., oval w/au gratin cover	6.00 – 7.00
Casserole, 2 qt., w/crystal knob cover	7.00 – 8.00
Casserole, 3 qt., double roaster	15.00 – 18.00
Custard, 5 oz.	1.50 – 2.00
Custard, 6 oz., deep	2.00 – 2.50
Custard, 6 oz., low	2.00 – 2.50

Dish, 11¾", oval, divided	4.00 – 5.00
Loaf pan, 5" x 9"	6.00 – 7.00
Measuring cup, 8 oz., black graduations	5.00 – 6.00
Measuring cup, 8 oz., red graduations	3.00 – 4.00
Measuring pitcher, 16 oz., black graduations	10.00 – 12.00
Measuring pitcher, 16 oz., red graduations	7.00 – 8.00
Measuring pitcher, 32 oz., black graduations	12.50 – 15.00
Measuring pitcher, 32 oz., red graduations	8.00 – 10.00
Percolator top	2.00 – 2.50
Pie dish, deep, 10 oz.	2.50 – 3.00
Pie dish, deep, 15 oz.	3.00 – 3.50
Pie pan, 8"	3.50 – 4.00
Pie pan, 9"	4.50 – 5.00
Pie pan, 9", deep dish	8.00 – 10.00
Pudding pan, 1 qt.	3.00 – 4.00
Table server	8.00 – 10.00
Utility dish, 6½" x 10½"	4.00 – 5.00
Utility dish, 8" x 12½"	5.00 – 6.00
Utility dish, 9½" x 14⅛"	6.00 – 7.00

Ovenware

"CURRIER & IVES" 1970s

Colors: Anchorwhite w/decal

Very little "Currier & Ives" Fire-King is marked. You have to know shapes and sizes. Every item found in "Blue Heaven" can also be found in "Currier and Ives"; look on page 184 for other types of items missing from the photo here. There were more glass companies that made "Currier & Ives" decorations. You will find Glasbake, Federal, and Hazel Atlas items. That's great if you are collecting "Currier & Ives," but a pain if you are only looking for Fire-King pieces.

I see more six ounce custards than anything, but mugs and chili bowls seem to be available. Mixing bowls and casseroles appear harder to find. Maybe they are still being used. Much of this ware was used as premiums for banks and groceries during the 1970s. That larger, 3½ quart mixing bowl was dropped from many of the later lines. The Chanticleer set may be the last one in which this bowl was included.

	White w/decal
Bowl, 5", chili	8.00 – 10.00
Bowl, mixing, 1 qt.	12.50 – 15.00
Bowl, mixing, 1½ qt.	18.00 – 20.00
Bowl, mixing, 2½ qt.	18.00 – 20.00
Cake pan, 8", square	12.00 – 15.00
Cake pan, 8", round	12.00 – 15.00
Casserole, 12 oz., hdld.	12.50 – 15.00
Casserole, 1 pt.	10.00 – 12.00
Casserole, 1 qt., w/crystal knob cover	10.00 – 12.00
Casserole, 1½ qt., oval w/au gratin cover	20.00 – 22.50
Casserole, 1½ qt., w/crystal knob cover	18.00 – 20.00
Casserole, 2 qt., w/crystal knob cover	20.00 – 22.50
Custard, 6 oz.	4.00 – 5.00
Loaf pan, deep, 5" x 9"	8.00 – 10.00
Mug, 8 oz.	8.00 – 10.00
Utility dish, 6½" x 10½"	12.00 – 15.00

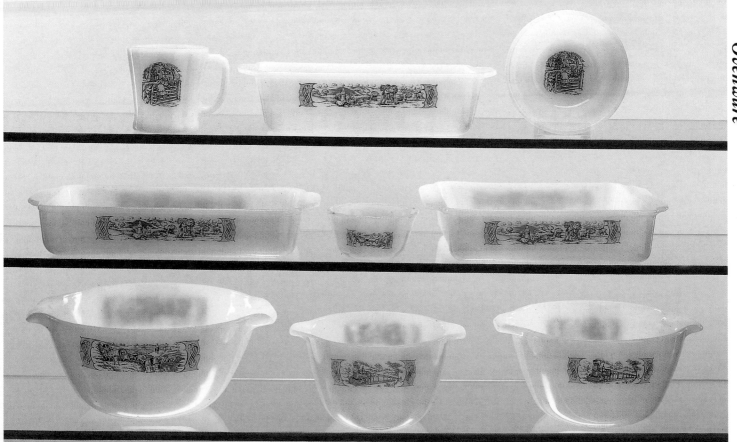

Ovenware

191

GAY FAD STUDIOS

Colors: Hand-decorated Anchorwhite and Ivory

Gay Fad Studios has become a byword for Fire-King collectors. That studio was located just across the street from Anchor Hocking's main plant. Their decorated Fire-King wares have caught the eye of enough serious collectors to swiftly push the price upward.

Most Gay Fad patterns are immediately obvious once you see a few of them. Remember that these pieces were hand painted; there will be design variations encountered! Designs are also subject to wear; chips in the paint are more easily found than you may wish. Apple designs have only been found on Ivory and satinized crystal. The Anchorwhite "Yellow Rose" and "Pine Cone" are found sporadically.

Page 194 and 195 show "Poinsettia" on Ivory and "Distlefink" on Anchorwhite. There are several variations of "Poinsettia." The term "Distlefink" has a Pennsylvania Dutch origin, but I am unsure who first called this bird pattern by that terminology.

Page 193 Apple, Yellow Rose, Ivy, Pine Cone

Row 1:	#1	Ivory, dessert, 5 oz.	12.50 – 15.00
	#2	Ivory, deep loaf pan	45.00 – 50.00
	#3	Ivory, individual baker, 6 oz.	12.50 – 15.00
Row 2:	#1	Ivory, 1½ qt. casserole	65.00 – 80.00
	#2	Ivory, 9" pie plate	40.00 – 45.00
	#3	Ivory, individual deep pie dish	20.00 – 25.00
Row 3:	#1	Ivory, 8", Swirl mixing bowl	50.00 – 65.00
	#2	Ivory, 9", Swirl mixing bowl	55.00 – 70.00
	#3	Ivory, 7", Swirl mixing bowl	50.00 – 65.00
		Same, 6" (not pictured)	50.00 – 65.00
Row 4:	#1	"Yellow Rose," Anchorwhite baking pan, 6½" x 10½"	50.00 – 60.00
	#2	"Yellow Rose," Anchorwhite deep loaf, 5" x 9"	45.00 – 50.00
	#3	"Pine Cone," Anchorwhite casserole, 1 pt.	40.00 – 50.00
	#4	"Yellow Rose," Anchorwhite casserole, 1 pt.	50.00 – 60.00
Row 5:	#1	"Ivy," Anchorwhite casserole, 1½ qt, oval, au gratin lid	50.00 – 60.00
	#2	"Ivy," Anchorwhite mixing bowl, 1 qt.	45.00 – 50.00
	#3	"Ivy," Anchorwhite mixing bowl, 1½ qt.	45.00 – 50.00
	#4	"Ivy," Anchorwhite casserole, 1 qt.	45.00 – 50.00

Page 194 Poinsettia, Poppy, Apple

Row 1:	#1	Red, 8", Swirl mixing bowl	45.00 – 50.00
	#2	Red, 9", Swirl mixing bowl	50.00 – 55.00
	#3	Red, 6", Swirl mixing bowl	40.00 – 45.00
Row 2:	#1	Red, casserole, 2 qt., lid only w/design	40.00 – 45.00
	#2	Red, dessert, 5 oz.	12.50 – 15.00
	#3,4	Red, comport, 6"	60.00 – 65.00
Row 3	:#1	Red, casserole, 2 qt.	60.00 – 65.00
	#2	Crystal, satinized, Apple 80 oz. ball jug	150.00 – 175.00
	#3	Red, casserole, 2 qt., lid only w/design	40.00 – 45.00
Row 4:	#1	Red, baking pan, 6½" x 10½"	35.00 – 40.00
	#2	Red, dessert, 5 oz.	12.50 – 15.00
	#3	Crystal, satinized, Apple tumbler	15.00 – 20.00
	#4	Red, deep loaf, 5" x 9"	35.00 – 40.00
Row 5:	#1	Red, casserole, 2 qt.	30.00 – 35.00
	#2	Red, cake pan, 8"	60.00 – 65.00
	#3	Red. pie plate, 9"	35.00 – 40.00

Page 195 Distlefink

Row 1	:#1	Red, 4" x 8", refrigerator container	60.00 – 65.00
	#2	Red, casserole, 2 qt.	70.00 – 75.00
	#3	Red, casserole, 1 pt.	50.00 – 55.00
Row 2:	#1	Blue, casserole, 1½ qt.	60.00 – 65.00
	#2	Blue or red, Splash Proof mixing bowl, 2 qt.	100.00 – 125.00
		Same, 1 qt. (not pictured)	150.00 – 200.00
		Same 3 qt. (see page 151)	100.00 – 125.00
		Same 4 qt. (not pictured)	100.00 – 125.00
Row 3:	#1	Red, baking pan, 6½" x 10½"	60.00 – 65.00
	#2	Red, deep loaf, 5" x 9"	65.00 – 70.00
Row 4:	#1	Red, casserole, 1½ qt, oval, au gratin lid	60.00 – 65.00
	#2	Red, Colonial Kitchen mixing bowl, 8¾"	100.00 – 125.00
	#3	4" x 4" refrigerator container	50.00 – 55.00

Ovenware

Ovenware

GAY FAD STUDIOS (CONT.)

I'm trying a different approach to pricing this section. Rather than pricing five pages line by line, I am going to list each item and price under its respective pattern. There may be an omission or two for items I have not confirmed existing; but the prices for a like item elsewhere should give you an idea of how to price anything I missed.

Gay Fad had a "Peach Blossom" pattern shown in their 1954 – 1955 catalog. It has been called "Dogwood" and "Apple Blossom" in the past. Peach blossoms have five petals; dogwood and apple blossoms, only four. "Peach Blossom" can be found on Federal and Hazel Atlas glass. "Outlined Fruit" is pictured at the top of page 199 and consists of an apple and blueberry. All lids are crystal unless otherwise noted.

At the bottom of page 200 are some newly discovered decorations from Gay Fad. Call that middle row "Dutch Tulip" for now and price as "Peach Blossom." Happy harvesting!

Ovenware

	FRUITS	OUTLINED FRUIT	PEACH BLOSSOM
Baking dish, 11¾", divided	30.00 – 35.00		
Baking pan, 6½" x 10½"	30.00 – 35.00	35.00 – 40.00	25.00 – 30.00
Batter bowl, handled w/spout	200.00 – 225.00		
Bowl, 5", cereal, straight side	12.50 – 15.00		
Bowl, 5", chili	12.50 – 15.00		10.00 – 12.00
Casserole, 1 pt.	25.00 – 30.00	35.00 – 40.00	25.00 – 30.00
Casserole, 1 qt.	25.00 – 30.00	40.00 – 45.00	25.00 – 30.00
Casserole, 1 qt., tab handles, white lid	40.00 – 45.00		40.00 – 45.00
Casserole, 12 oz., French, handled	*10.00 – 12.00		15.00 – 20.00
Casserole, 1½ qt.	30.00 – 35.00	25.00 – 30.00	20.00 – 25.00
Casserole, 1½ qt., oval, au gratin lid	35.00 – 40.00		25.00 – 30.00
Casserole, 1½ qt., oval, au gratin white lid			40.00 – 45.00
Casserole, 2 qt.	30.00 – 35.00	55.00 – 60.00	25.00 – 30.00
Creamer, stacking	20.00 – 25.00		
Cruet (satinized crystal)		8.00 – 10.00	
Custard, 5 oz.	8.00 – 10.00		6.00 – 8.00
Custard, 6 oz.	8.00 – 10.00		6.00 – 8.00
Grease jar	100.00 – 125.00		
Loaf pan, 5" x 9", deep	25.00 – 30.00	35.00 – 40.00	20.00 – 25.00
Mixing bowl, 2 qt., w/gold leaf, FEDERAL			15.00 – 20.00
Mixing bowl, 3 qt., w/gold leaf, FEDERAL			15.00 – 20.00
Mixing bowl, Colonial Kitchen, 6"	12.50 – 15.00		14.00 – 16.00
Mixing bowl, Colonial Kitchen, 7³⁄₁₆"	14.00 – 16.00		16.00 – 18.00
Mixing bowl, Colonial Kitchen, 8¾"	16.00 – 18.00		18.00 – 20.00
Mixing bowl, Splash Proof, 1 qt.	85.00 – 90.00	150.00 – 175.00	
Mixing bowl, Splash Proof, 2 qt.	65.00 – 75.00	85.00 – 90.00	
Mixing bowl, Splash Proof, 3 qt.	65.00 – 75.00	85.00 – 90.00	
Mixing bowl, Splash Proof, 4 qt.	65.00 – 75.00	85.00 – 90.00	
Mixing bowl, tab handled, 1 qt.	60.00 – 65.00		
Mixing bowl, tab handled, 1½ qt.	45.00 – 50.00		
Mixing bowl, tab handled, 2½ qt.	50.00 – 55.00		
Mug, 8 oz.	8.00 – 10.00		10.00 – 12.00
Mug, 8 oz., stacking	12.50 – 15.00		
Pan, cake, 8" x 8", square	25.00 – 30.00	30.00 – 35.00	25.00 – 30.00
Refrigerator, 4" x 4", square	12.50 – 15.00	25.00 – 30.00	12.50 – 15.00
Refrigerator, 4" x 8", rectangular	15.00 – 18.00	30.00 – 35.00	15.00 – 18.00
Refrigerator, 4¼", round, "star burst" lid			20.00 – 25.00
Refrigerator, 4¼", x 9", oval, "star burst" lid			30.00 – 35.00
Relish, 13", 3-part, Lace Edge	75.00 – 80.00		
Shakers, pr. (satinized crystal)		12.50 – 15.00	
Sugar, stacking	20.00 – 25.00		

* Banana 40.00 – 45.00   Purple grape 12.50 – 15.00   Orange slice, green grape 15.00 – 18.00

IVORY AND IVORY WHITE 1948 – MID 1950s

Ivory ovenware was first shown in Anchor Hocking's Catalog L, released in 1948. The introduction states "Ivory Fire-King is a new QUALITY product — a revelation in glass making — the only oven glass line ever produced which adequately complements chinaware." To combat new china issues that were eroding some of Anchor Hocking's market, it further stated it has "the warm Ivory color of semi-porcelain and the translucence of china. It will not check or craze as it is the same glass all the way through."

Catalog L was devoted to Fire-King: Ivory, Jade-ite, and Sapphire. Sapphire encompassed "Oven-Glass" and dinnerware ("Bubble"). Jade-ite dinnerware featured "Jane Ray" and the rest of the Jade-ite was kitchenware and novelty items.

Ivory ovenware is found in two shades. A later version was produced as Ivory White and a boxed set of that is pictured below. I have priced Ivory White in the listing below, although some pieces are not shown on page 203. Ivory White is more scarce than Ivory, but it has not been pursued by Fire-King collectors the way Ivory has been.

There are four sizes of knobbed lid casseroles in Ivory, with the larger casserole having been sold in baking sets. Very little use for the pint-sized casserole was evidently found in kitchens back then, because they are rarely found now.

The first item in the bottom row has an embossed Fire-King ("Philbe") design on the pie plate lid as well as the bottom. The two quart casserole lids are sometimes found embossed Fire-King. That lid is scarce compared to non-embossed lids.

Page 203 Ivory (unless noted)

Row 1:	#1	Pie dish, 5⅜", individual	12.00 – 15.00
	#2	Casserole, 2 qt.	20.00 – 25.00
		Same, with decal decoration #253	40.00 – 50.00
		Lid only, embossed Fire-King	20.00 – 22.50
	#3	Table server	15.00 – 17.50
	#4	Casserole, 1 pt.	27.50 – 30.00
		Same, Ivory White	8.00 – 10.00
Row 2:	#1	Pie pan, 9"	8.00 – 10.00
		Same, Ivory White	7.00 – 8.00
		Pie pan, 8", Ivory White	20.00 – 22.50
	#2	Dessert, 5 oz.	4.00 – 5.00
	#3	Cake pan, 9"	12.00 – 15.00
Row 3:	#1	Custard cup, 6 oz., deep	5.00 – 6.00
	#2	Baker, 6 oz., individual	4.00 – 5.00
	#3	Casserole, 1½ qt.	18.00 – 20.00
	#4	Baking pan, 6½" x 10½"	16.00 – 18.00
Row 4:	#1	Casserole, 1 qt., pie plate lid (emb. Fire-King "Philbe" design)	175.00 – 200.00
	#2	Casserole, 1 qt.	25.00 – 27.50
		Same, Ivory White	8.00 – 10.00
	#3	Loaf pan, deep, 9⅜"	12.00 – 15.00

Jade-ite ovenware prices have made huge gains in the last two years. The only problem with that is **new** collectors are balking at some of the prices being asked. There apparently are no records definitely answering when Jade-ite was first made. Jade-ite first appears in the 1946 Anchor Hocking catalog; and, by 1948, their catalog was full of Jade-ite.

Most of those rare pieces shown in the first book are even more scarce, today, due to collectors buying them up and salting them away in their sets. A couple of Jade-ite casseroles have been on the market, but were quickly snapped up by eager buyers. Custard cups are being found in sets of six, but they sell very quickly. Six ruffled top custards turned up in northern Kentucky last June.

A bouillon, or handless cup, is pictured here. This sold through an Internet auction where the buzz was that it was a piece of newly made glass from Martha Stewart's Fenton collection. It evidently wasn't new; but, what was its original purpose? (See p. 156, 157.)

There are two small, handled bowls without spouts being found occasionally. One of these is like the 12 ounce French casseroles found with lids in other ovenware patterns. It is 5" in diameter, 7" counting the handle. The other handled custard is 6" (with handle) and a shade under 5" in diameter. These are being found in groups of four, so they must have been sold in sets for whatever purpose.

I have listed all the measurements for the custards and bowls shown in case you should spot a Jade-ite mystery piece. Remember, most Jade-ite ovenware is hard to find.

Page 205 Jade-ite

Row	#	Description	Price Low	Price High
Row 1:	#1	Custard, deep, ruffled top	250.00 –	300.00
	#2	Handled custard, 4⁵⁄₁₆" (6" w/handle)	400.00 –	450.00
	#3	French casserole, 5" (7" w/handle), w/lid	450.00 –	500.00
	#4	Lid for casserole	4.00 –	5.00
Row 2:	#1	Ribbed custard, 3⁵⁄₈" x 1⁹⁄₁₆" deep	100.00 –	150.00
	#2	Custard, 3⁵⁄₈" x 1⁵⁄₈" deep	100.00 –	125.00
	#3	Casserole, Swirled, 7"	morgue	
	#4	Baker, 5" x 1½" deep	100.00 –	125.00
	#5	Casserole, 1½ qt.	1,500.00 –	2,000.00
Row 3:	#1	Skillet, 7", 2 spout	140.00 –	165.00
	#2	Custard, 6 oz., individual	65.00 –	70.00
		Set of six in wire holder	400.00 –	450.00
	#3	4½" x 5" jar (catalog description) (lid 20.00)	35.00 –	40.00
Row 4:	#1	Skillet, 7", 1 spout	70.00 –	80.00
	#2	Pie plate, 9"	175.00 –	200.00
	#3	Loaf pan, 5" x 9"	45.00 –	50.00

Ovenware

NATURE'S BOUNTY 1976 – 1978

Colors: Anchorwhite w/decal

Nature's Bounty is just being discovered by collectors. Prices, at present, remain rather reasonable compared to other patterns. It has been less than 25 years since this pattern was introduced; there may well be a lot of it still being used. Dishes seem to re-circulate in about 20 year cycles. If mom used this and you are starting to set up a household, she might start you out with a piece or two from her pantry. First thing you know, you like it and search for more. Welcome to collecting!

	White w/decal
Bowl, mixing, 1 qt.	8.00 – 10.00
Bowl, mixing, 1½ qt.	10.00 – 12.00
Bowl, mixing, 2½ qt.	12.50 – 15.00
Bowl, mixing, 3½ qt.	15.00 – 18.00
Cake pan, 8", square	9.00 – 10.00
Cake pan, 8", round	9.00 – 10.00
Casserole, 1 pt.	10.00 – 12.50
Casserole, 1 qt., w/crystal knob cover	10.00 – 12.00
Casserole, 1½ qt., oval w/au gratin cover	12.50 – 15.00
Casserole, 1½ qt., w/crystal knob cover	12.50 – 15.00
Casserole, 2 qt., w/crystal knob cover	12.50 – 15.00
Casserole, 3 qt., w/crystal knob cover	15.00 – 18.00
Custard, 6 oz.	3.00 – 4.00
Loaf pan, deep, 5" x 9"	8.00 – 10.00
Loaf pan, lid	15.00 – 20.00
Mug, 8 oz.	5.00 – 6.00
Utility dish, 6½" x 10½"	8.00 – 10.00
Utility dish, 8" x 12½"	10.00 – 12.00

Ovenware

"PHILBE" (FIRE-KING DESIGN)

Colors: Ivory and Jade-ite

The top row below consists of refrigerator containers, not truly ovenware; but they are Jade-ite pieces found with the raised "Philbe" design that thrills collectors. The prices for Jade-ite containers have increased in the last two years, but not as dramatically as some of the other Jade-ite items. That is probably due to the fact that the embossed line had already had tremendous price hikes before the first book was finished. If you look back three years, prices were a much different story. This "Philbe" line of Jade-ite was the first to rocket in price.

Prices for the juice saver pie plate have also been spiraling upward. Actually, all embossed Jade-ite prices have been escalating!

Did you know there are three styles of embossed custard cups? I only knew of two. A newly found one is pictured above. In the bottom row below, the first mug has the embossed "Philbe" design, but the second does not. These mugs are shaped differently than the normally found Jade-ite mug. Look at the handles for starters. The base is flat and not indented as the regularly found mugs.

The "Philbe" Ivory casserole with pie plate lid is also pictured in the Ivory section!

Above		Custard, 6 oz., individual	350.00 – 400.00
Below		Ivory casserole, 1 qt., pie plate lid	175.00 – 200.00
Row 1:	#1,2	Refrigerator container and lid, 5⅛" x 9½"	65.00 – 75.00
	#3	Refrigerator container and lid, 4½" x 5"	35.00 – 40.00
Row 2:	#1	Custard or dessert, 5 oz	150.00 – 200.00
	#2	Custard or individual baker, 6 oz	150.00 – 200.00
	#3	Pie plate, Juice Saver, 10⅜"	325.00 – 350.00
	#4	Mug, 8 oz.	100.00 – 125.00
	#5	Same mug, no design	20.00 – 25.00

SAPPHIRE BLUE, 1941 – 1956

Fire-King Sapphire Blue is the most recognized Fire-King pattern. Grandmas and mothers for generations have used this ovenware. I grew up with Mom always making bread pudding from scratch in half a large roaster. She couldn't, or wouldn't, use anything else.

Whenever Fire-King is mentioned, it is this Sapphire that a majority of people call to mind. Jade-ite is gaining ground, but there are other companies' jade colors which tend to confuse the uninitiated in glass collecting. Fire-King has always been recognized for its durability; and thus, so has Sapphire. Sapphire is excellent for standard ovens, but it has an inclination to develop heat cracks from sudden temperature changes when used in today's microwaves. After all, it wasn't designed for microwave use. We cracked a few bowls fixing instant oatmeal before we gave up and switched to Turquoise Blue. Let our mishaps suffice, so you will not have to lose a piece that way.

Page 209 pictures some ordinary pieces except for the juice saver pie plate and large utility pan in row 2. The first bowl in row 3 was made for Kroger in 1944 and holds 19⅛ ounces according to a label found at Anchor Hocking. Only a few have been seen thus far. That skillet in row 4 is one of the most desirable pieces of Sapphire.

Page 210, row 1, starts with a **dry measure** which holds eight ounces and **has no spout**. Be aware that a few spouted measuring cups have been ground down and passed off as dry measures. The second row has a percolator top and an easily found 6 ounce custard next to it. All other pieces in that row are rare. The small funnel is from Anchor Hocking, but others could surface once you know how it is shaped. Next to the funnel are custard cups. The first holds 19½ ounces, and the next, 12 ounces. Ironically, I had just bought a 12 ounce custard in Lancaster before I visited Anchor Hocking's morgue where I discovered a lid for the custard that was dated December 1944. Both morgue pieces were marked "Sample only."

Note the non-designed table server on page 212. Few plain **Sapphire** ones have been seen! The Sunny Suzy sets fetch $150.00 to $175.00 in a nice box. That Binkys set with funnel was priced in the Children's Dishes (page 167). The box of Binkys Nip Caps is worth $50.00 by itself. Two views of a Fyrock nurser show how it was shaped to keep it from rolling. The Tuffy nurser says "Coldproof" on one side and "Heatproof" on the other.

Page 213 shows a lid (morgue piece) which was tested at ⅓ blue color on November 26, 1940. Row 2 shows the inside of a "Diamond" salt bowl, the bottom of a cut design, 6 ounce baker, and a Fyrock casserole (morgue piece). The bottom row shows two Silex dripolators believed by collectors to be Fire-King; I cannot prove it. Only the lid is Fire-King on that Bersted Mfg. Co. popcorn popper.

The top of page 214 shows two views of a whimsy dish and two styles of cereals. The bottom left shows a couple of cut designs on Sapphire while the middle shows the half roaster which was set beside the cake pan for comparison. (There are no raised ridges of glass on the tabs of the cake pan.) The bottom right shows three styles of custards and a "thin" mug when compared to the regular mug.

Ovenware

Item	Price
Baker, 1 pt., 4½" x 5"	7.00 – 8.00
Baker, 1 pt., 5⅝", round	6.00 – 8.00
Baker, 1 qt., 7¼", round	10.00 – 12.00
Baker, 1½ qt., 8¼", round	14.00 – 16.00
Baker, 2 qt., 8⅞", round	14.00 – 16.00
Bowl, 4⅜", individual pie plate	20.00 – 22.00
Bowl, 4⅝", 2", high, three bands	morgue
Bowl, 5⅜", cereal or deep dish pie plate	20.00 – 22.00
Bowl, 5⁷⁄₁₆", 2¹¹⁄₁₆" deep (Kroger 12/30/44)	350.00 – 400.00
Bowl, measuring-mixing, 16 oz.	25.00 – 27.50
Cake pan, 8¾", no tabs	40.00 – 45.00
Casserole, 10 oz., 4¾", individual	11.00 – 13.00
Casserole, 1 pt., knob handle cover, 5⅝"	12.00 – 14.00
Casserole, 1 qt., knob handle cover, 7¼"	16.00 – 18.00
Casserole, 1 qt., pie plate cover	16.00 – 18.00
Casserole, 1½ qt., knob handle cover, 8¼"	20.00 – 22.00
Casserole, 1½ qt., pie plate cover	18.00 – 20.00
Casserole, 2 qt., knob handle cover, 8⅞"	20.00 – 22.00
Casserole, 2 qt., pie plate cover	22.50 – 25.00
Cup, 8 oz. measuring, 1 spout	20.00 – 22.00
Cup, 8 oz., dry measure, no spout	850.00 – 900.00
Cup, 8 oz., measuring, 3 spout	28.00 – 30.00
Custard cup or baker, 5 oz.	4.00 – 5.00
Custard cup or baker, 6 oz., shallow	4.00 – 5.00
Custard cup or baker, 6 oz., (not pictured, no design)	12.00 – 15.00
Custard cup or baker, 6 oz., 3⅜" deep	5.00 – 6.00
Custard cup or baker, 12 oz., 4¹⁄₁₆" deep	350.00 – 400.00
Custard cup lid for 12 oz. (12/44)	morgue
Custard cup or baker, 19½ oz., 4¾" deep	morgue
Loaf pan, 9⅛" x 5⅛", deep	20.00 – 22.00
Funnel	morgue
Mug, coffee, 7 oz., thick	25.00 – 28.00
Mug, coffee, 7 oz., thin	40.00 – 45.00
Nipple cover	240.00 – 265.00
Nurser, 4 oz.	18.00 – 20.00
Nurser, 8 oz.	30.00 – 35.00
Nurser, 8 oz., Fyrock	35.00 – 40.00
Nurser, 8 oz., "Tuffy" Heatproof/Coldproof	30.00 – 35.00
Percolator top, 2⅛"	4.00 – 5.00
Pie plate, 8⅜", 1½" deep	7.00 – 9.00
Pie plate, 9", 1½" deep	8.00 – 10.00
Pie plate, 9⅝", 1½" deep	8.00 – 10.00
Pie plate, 10⅜", juice saver	135.00 – 150.00
Popcorn popper	35.00 – 40.00
Refrigerator jar & cover, 4½" x 5"	12.50 – 15.00
Refrigerator jar & cover, 5⅛" x 9⅛"	30.00 – 32.50
Roaster, 8¾"	50.00 – 55.00
Roaster, 10⅜"	75.00 – 80.00
Skillet, 7", w/4⅝" handle	500.00 – 600.00
Silex, 2 cup dripolator (without insert $20.00)	35.00 – 40.00
Silex, 6 cup coffee dripolator	175.00 – 225.00
Table server, tab handles (w/design)	20.00 – 22.00
Table server, tab handles (no design)	60.00 – 70.00
Utility bowl, 6⅞", 1 qt.	16.00 – 18.00
Utility bowl, 8⅜", 1½ qt.	18.00 – 20.00
Utility bowl, 10⅛", 2 qt.	20.00 – 22.00
Utility pan, 8⅛" x 12½"	90.00 – 100.00
Utility pan, 10½" x 2" deep	22.50 – 25.00

Ovenware

FIRE - KING OVEN GLASS

Housewives prefer to cook in glass for they are then able to actually see their foods cooking, eliminating the possibility of improperly cooked foods. Glass is also more easily cleaned than metal utensils, saving time and labor.

A three-fold purpose—bake, serve, and store in the same dish. Fire-King oven glass is not only suitable for oven cooking but makes ideal serving dishes for the table and in addition is safe and practical for refrigerator use.

Not only does Fire-King possess unusual cooking qualities but it is attractive, a complement to any table, and above all—the lowest priced oven glass on the market.

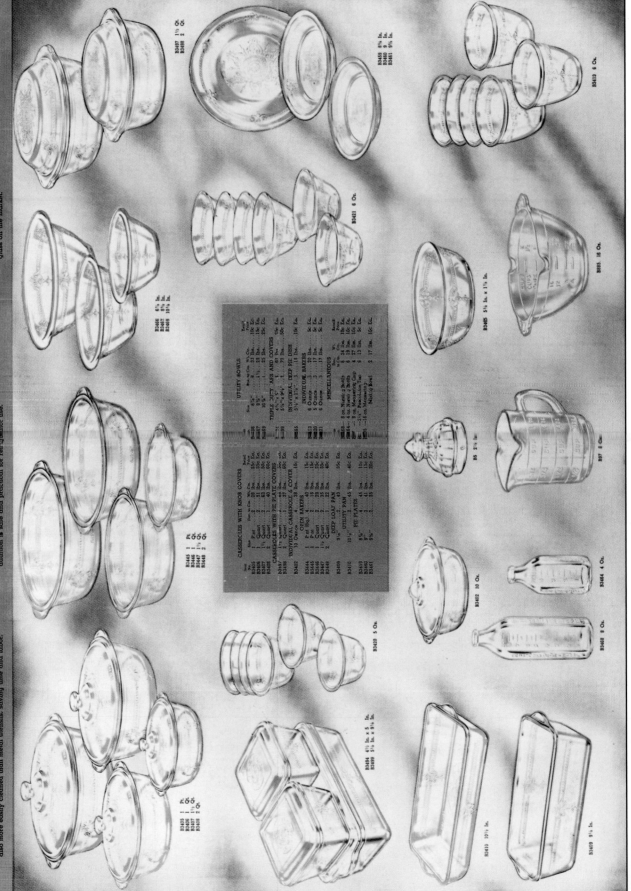

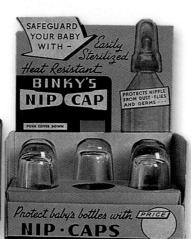

Ovenware

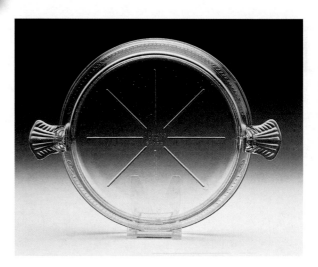

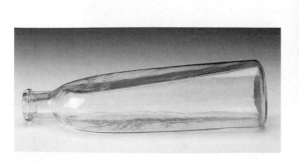

Ovenware

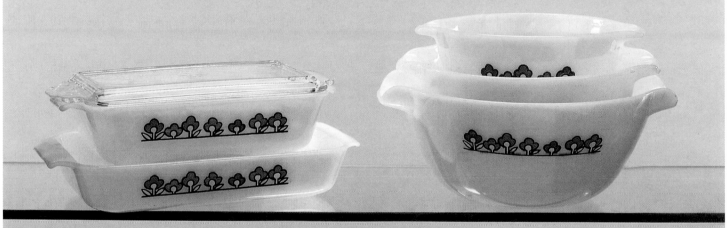

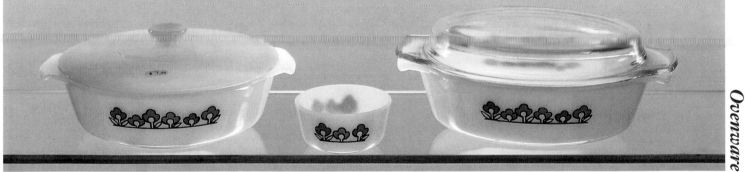

Above: Breakfast bowl, $110.00; chili bowl, $15.00
Right: Turquoise Blue chili or cereal bowl, $15.00;
        thin cereal bowl, $45.00; berry bowl, $10.00
Below: Beaded edge small mixing bowl, $22.00;
        15 oz. deep bowl, $28.00; 10 oz. breakfast, $28.00

Above: Restaurant Ware flat rimmed soup, $110.00;
        "Jane Ray" flat rimmed soup, $250.00
Left: Beaded edge small mixing bowl $22.00;
        10 oz. breakfast bowl, $28.00
Below: "Jane Ray" flat rimmed soup, $250.00;
        "Jane Ray" regular flat soup, $24.00

Row 1:   St. Denis cup and saucer, $20.00; Ransom cup and saucer, $25.00; Restaurant Ware cup and saucer, $15.00; Shell cup and saucer, $15.00; Swirl cup and saucer, $60.00

Row 2:   Anchor Hocking straight tumblers, $10.00 ea.; Hazel Atlas tumbler in middle (smaller base than top), $8.00; White color, $15; Ivory White, $10.00; Ivory, $12.00

Row 3:   Child's mug, $250.00; tall 8½ oz. mug, $20.00; 8 oz. mug, $8.00; tall 8½ oz. mug, $20.00; punch mug, $5.00

Platters, Below: 11½", $50.00; 9½", $55.00; 8⅞" oval without indent, $85.00; 9¾" "football," $70.00

Row 1: Jade-ite mug, Masonic Lodge, $20.00
Jade-ite mug, Fleet Aircraft Service Squadron #12, $25.00
Jade-ite Restaurant Ware plate with Holly dated 1978, $20.00
Jade-ite Charm berry bowl, decorated, $35.00
Jade-ite "Deco" decal decorated vase, $30.00

Row 2: Jade-ite one spout skillet w/label, $125.00
Jade-ite Shell dinner plate w/35¢ sticker, $30.00
Jade-ite "Deco" vase applied decorations, $30.00

Row 3: Crystal shakers with stripes, $12.00 ea.
Jade-ite lopsided cup and saucer, $10.00

Row 4: Embossed 15" turkey platter, $22.00

ADDENDUM 2

Row 1: Anchorwhite relish with flamingo and palm tree, $20.00; Anchorwhite relish with roses in box, $20.00
Row 2: 22K egg plate with label in box $15.00; Jade-ite ice bucket, $125.00
Row 3: Ivory Beaded Edge bowls and grease set in box $125.00

⚓ THE END

The two sets of creamers and sugars below were found after our major photography session in October, but I had to make room for them because they were so unusual. Enjoy!

Shown on page 223 are some metal tops to illustrate how condition affects price.

Row 1: P shaker top, $12.00; S shaker top, $15.00; Tulip grease top, $10.00
Row 2: Tulip Pepper top, $10.00
Row 3: Tulip Pepper top, $15.00; Tulip Salt top, $20.00; Tulip grease top, $20.00
Below: Wheat creamer and sugar with advertising, $50.00 set; "Distlefink" on Prescut "Pineapple" sugar, $50.00; "Distlefink" on Prescut "Pineapple" creamer, $50.00; Fire-King Cookbook, $75.00 – 100.00.

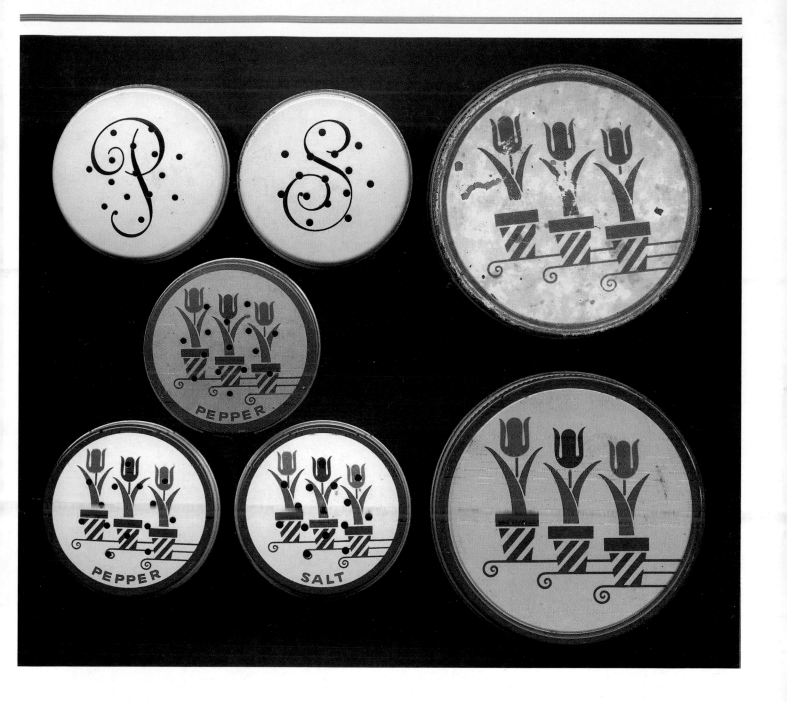

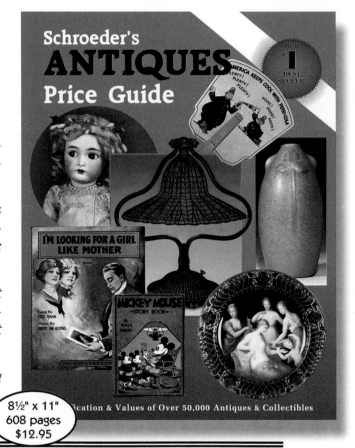